Why RACE Matters

ISBN-13: 978-1500826994

ISBN-10: 1500826995

Why RACE Matters

Table of Contents

Chapter 1 – Race and racism

Section 1 - What is race?

The general consensus among current day anthropologists is "race" is a cultural construct and does not exist as a scientific fact or genetic variation. Their rationalization is that variation among individuals is far greater than between subgroups of *Homo sapiens* such as ethnic groups. This is primarily a politically correct motivated position by the professional anthropological and archaeological associations whose members are often funded by universities who receive federal funding who have conditions in place in regards to non-discrimination. It's an illusion to bury the evidence and facts. Perhaps anthropological groups worry that the paltry numbers of black anthropologists might subject their profession to accusations of racial bias, but if race doesn't exist, then racism cannot be a factor why there are few black anthropologists and archaeologists.

Anyone with eyes open wide must recognize there are races among human beings, with lineages that can be traced both through archaeological evidence and DNA sequencing. Racial and ethnic differences are expressed not only in the difference in skin color, but other measurable differences that are generalized among various groups in higher proportions than in other groups that possess less of the genetic traits expressed as phenotypic attributes.

For example, most Asians possess Type O positive blood (90%+) while white Europeans have a greater distribution of Type A negative blood. Asians also have smaller stature and bone structure as compared to most African or European lineages, and the typical shape of the Asian skull is markedly different from white or black groups in the slope of the forehead, width and length of the nose, width versus length of the skull, shape of the jaw and prominence of the brow ridge in addition to the shape of the face (more circular), shape of the eyes, depth of the eye socket, distance between the eyes, and other distinguishing genetically evolved traits from environmental adaptations of their early ancestors.

So despite the politically correct position taken by anthropologists, as far as what almost all people in the world perceive, race exists. The fact that a light skin person can get a suntan or a dark skin person can lighten their skin using various chemical products doesn't change a person's race. Instead, what you end up with is a tanned white person like actor David Niven or a light skin singer like Michael Jackson. The fact that Michael Jackson had obvious plastic surgeries to whiten his nose and used chemicals to lighten his skin didn't change him from a "Negroid" to a "Caucasoid" and both black and white people will swear that Michael Jackson was born a black man and he died a black man.

Anthropologists are attempting to create an illusion that race does not exist, however any person on the street can distinguish between people of different races, except perhaps for mixed-race individuals whose genotype has become hybridized. Simple comparison is to recognize there are "pure breeds" of dogs and mixed breeds, or mutts. The same applies to humans. Where there are individuals whose genetic lineage reflects no breeding outside

4

of their DNA pool, then their racial characteristics remain static. Consequently, Swedish people whose families have only interbred with Swedes will likely look light skinned, have blond hair, blue eyes and "Aryan" features, and look different from Asians or Africans.

Let's stop pretending there's no such thing as race. The rare exception to racial phenotypes does not negate the larger generalized factual observations and DNA evidence that prove gene clusters exists for the different "pure" races that make them markedly different from each other. The evidence for race is in plain site, and the mixture of individuals from the three primary races produce hybrids that generally exhibit mid-ground phenotypes from the parents. The reason so many African-Americas are lighter skinned than Africans is due to the fact that during the two-hundred and fifty years of slavery that spanned 25-30 generations, the blood of white "masters" intermingled with a certain percentage of the black nannies and housemaids, who were after all considered "property" and didn't have any legal rights. Black men who were slaves were also mixing with the slave masters' wives and daughters in secret (but hanged when discovered when guilt ridden wives confessed that once they had black, they didn't want to go back).

Section 2 – Natural genetic racism

Now that we have established the fact that race exists as an obvious observable phenomenon that is based on the phenotypic expression of genetic differences that occur between subgroups of human beings, labeled as races, let's deal with the controversy in how different cultures view and treat racially different individuals and groups... the issue of racism.

Human beings are animals, and in many ways our natural drives, fears and behaviors reflect that exhibited by other mammals. Let's look at some of these universal behavior propensities common to almost all animals:

- Search for food and water – Insufficient food and water results in weakened individuals, who then are more likely to fall prey to stronger competitors and predators.
- Fear of predators – Those without a reasonable level of fear, a false sense of security ensues that increases the probability of exposure to dangerous predators that can result serious injuries and therefore death.
- Fear of the unknown – People without apprehension of the unknown and unfamiliar, there is no exercise of caution that results in a lack of concern and awareness of the environment that could have predators in hiding.
- Need for shelter – Exposure to the elements subject individuals to great discomforts and extremes that wear the body down, stress out the immune system and make them visible to predators.
- Reproductive impulses – An insufficient birth rate over deaths results to eventual species extinction. Unfortunately, as most other species are dying off, humans continue to reproduce much faster than they are dying.
- Familial affinity – Without the protection family, young individuals easily fall prey to larger stronger predators. Family members also give the love and nurturing most that mammals need when they are developing.

- Social interaction – Humans are primarily social animals and need the interaction and affection of other people. However, as many people are toxic predators and exploiters, it's often less drama and vulnerability to avoid most people you don't already know well and like. In the olden days, people were more honest and cooperative and there was a sense of community and the common good that is lacking in modern society.

- Activity – Animals are usually active in search of food when not resting or hiding from predators. In humans, boredom is the primary motivation for people to do things once their bellies are full. Most people can't handle boredom because their brains start working overtime and then they feel like sleeping. People who keep moderately active seem to have less mental and emotional issues that can be caused by too much thinking and not enough activity.

- Territoriality – Wild animals feel compelled to mark their territory with their scent. People do the same, but instead of urinating to claim territory rights, they sign documents to take ownership of houses, cars, and spouses.

- Dominance – The animal world is based entirely on dominance and submission in a hierarchical structure that pervades almost every species, and particularly in human civilizations where the "Alpha males" dominate.

- Violence – The most fundamental survival instinct after searching for food and water is violence. Before the advent of civilizations and the social order created by dominant males, there was a lot more conflict and fighting. With the establishment of the social pecking order, the Apex Predator

- almost always wins until he gets too old to beat up or kill his challengers. This phenomenon of the fittest replacing the "has beens" is common in the animal kingdom, but with humans, the system of monetary wealth permits "old farts" who probably can't get an erection even with Viagra, to keep in their company the most attractive symbols of male virility… buxom blondes.

- Rest and sleep – These fundamental instinctive drives serves to renew cellular and mental processes, without which the toxins in the body are not expelled and health issues would eventually ensue. When animals become physically weakened by lack of cellular repair and regeneration, they become more susceptible to predators who tend to keep in top form in order to survive the hunt.

- Discrimination – All animals and humans do it. Ever notice that birds of a feather flock together? It's not by accident, but by evolutionary genetic design for both procreative and sustainability reasons. Humans segregate themselves by race, ethnicity, social class, religion, and an assortment of reasons that provide a sense of familiarity and security. If we remove the cultural norms and influence of wealth and the governments they control, we would find people tend to seek familiarity because that gives them a sense of comfort, safety, predictability and continuity. Consequently, without

- legal intervention and media influence, people naturally segregate themselves into racial, ethnic, and social subgroups. Isn't that obvious?

In nature, all newborns automatically imprint on their parents and develop the needed discrimination ability to discern family from foe... friendly from predators. Humans have this same genetic propensity... infants imprint on their mothers or their caretakers, recognize and become comfortable with the racial appearance of whoever gives them food, comfort and security. No wonder if white children are raised around whites, blacks by blacks, and so on, those children feel most comfortable and safer around people of their own race. Why is it that even with existing government laws against "red lining" or not selling homes to non-whites in all white neighborhoods, that the vast majority of people prefer to live among others from their own race and ethnic groups? De facto segregation is real even if it's not government policy as in the past. Racial preference is real, even though miscegenation laws have been expunge from the books since WW2 in most places in America. Why is American still divided in racial lines? Because it's natural. Let's stop pretending racism is rare, when in fact it's the prevailing rule. People tend to associate and give preference to those who they feel comfortable with, who share physical commonalities such as ethnicity and race. Whites prefer to be around whites, blacks around blacks, Asians around Asians, and so on. It's no wonder over 95% of nation-states are comprised of people who are almost unanimous homogenous racial and ethnic demographics. If you don't believe that, who are 95% of the residents of Japan, Korea(s), Finland, Australia, Nigeria, Israel, Serbia, Saudi Arabia, and so on? It's only in the U.S.A. and China where significant racial and ethnic minorities exist, as the rest of the global pie are cut up into slices of homogeneous groups based on racial and ethnic identities.

Distribution of U.S. Population by Race/Ethnicity, 2010

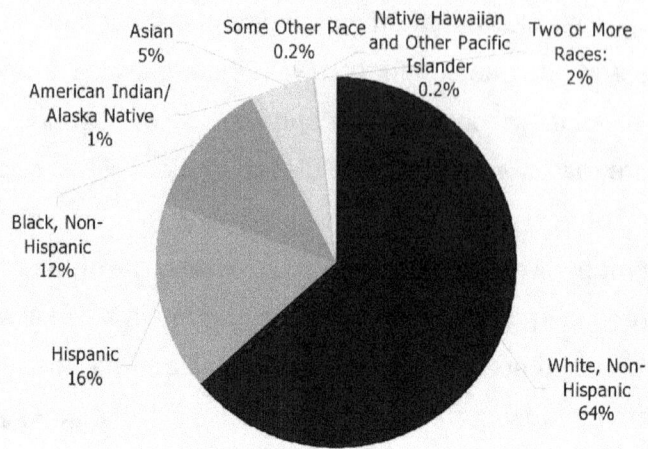

Asian
5%

American Indian/
Alaska Native
1%

Some Other Race
0.2%

Native Hawaiian
and Other Pacific
Islander
0.2%

Two or More
Races:
2%

Black, Non-
Hispanic
12%

Hispanic
16%

White, Non-
Hispanic
64%

Total U.S. Population = 308.7 million

SOURCE: 2010 U.S. Census

China's 56 Ethnic Groups

China officially registers 56 ethnic groups. The ethnic Chinese, known as the Han Chinese, compose 92 percent of the population. Han Chinese speak seven languages, with Mandarin or Putonghua – which means "common speech" -- being the official and most-used. Cantonese, which is spoken in Hong Kong and in China's other southern provinces, is the second most popular. Most of the 55 other ethnic groups use their own languages.

China's minorities account for a small 8 percent of the entire population. They live along the country's borders and some of them live on both sides.

China has five Autonomous Regions for its minorities: Guangxi, Xinjiang, Tibet, Inner Mongolia and Ningxia.

Chinese has high numbers of Chinese troops stationed in Tibet, Xinjiang and along the border provinces. The Western powers have attempted many times to separate these areas from China ever since early 19th Century. The independent groups are based in USA and supported mainly by the American political parties.

China was ruled by Han most of the time in the past except in Yuen Dynasty that Mongols ruled for less than 100 years and in Qing Dynasty, Manchuria ruled for almost 300 years. China's boundary today was solidified in early Qing Dynasty in early 17th Century.

China is a multi-culture and multi-disciplined society for a few thousand years. All minorities in China today have the equal right as Han Chinese. Since minorities reside in the remote area and usually poor, Chinese government has preference policy to provide training for the minorities to progress, govern and manage.

Chinese would like to enjoy the peaceful environment and definitely can accommodate all religions and nationalities if there is no foreign interference.

Powerpoint by Oei Hui Kiat, Singapore, Early July 2009.

Section 3 – Cultural racism

Human beings possess all of the behavioral tendencies common to almost all mammals and non-human primates. However, unlike other animals, humans possess a comparatively well-developed brain that allows them to create culture as an adaptive strategy to their environment. Culture comprises all of the social rules, political system, subsistence and economic system, migratory behavior, and technologies that allowed groups of individuals to beneficially adapt to their environments and to adjust to environmental changes, least become extinct like the Neanderthal and Cro-Magnon cousins of *Homo sapiens.*

It is in mankind's ability to create culture that enabled the development of racism, or treating individuals and subgroups differently based upon their perceived races. Other than skin color being the most obvious trait that can be seen from a distance, it caused racism to be primarily based on the most observable trait because it is easily recognizable and distinguishes individuals from one race to that of another. Racially hybridized individuals are a more recent phenomenon after removal of legal miscegenation barriers during the past century, along with the greater international mobility of people from different races, ethnic groups and cultures to interact and intermingle. As a greater number of mixed-race individuals will eventually be born, the issues of race and racism may lose its cultural significance, but that is likely another century away.

Racism is not only the identification of individuals from the different major races based on genetic make up that reflects the geographic origins of their original ancestors, it's the different values that society and people place on each race as compared to another. For example, in the book, 1984 by George Orwell, the society controlled by the state, Big Brother, had institutionalized the different races into a caste system, labeled as the Alphas, Betas, Gamma, Delta and Epsilon. Each level of the caste system reflected a variation of racial make-up and socioeconomic status... not unlike the caste system traditionally in place in India as illustrated below:

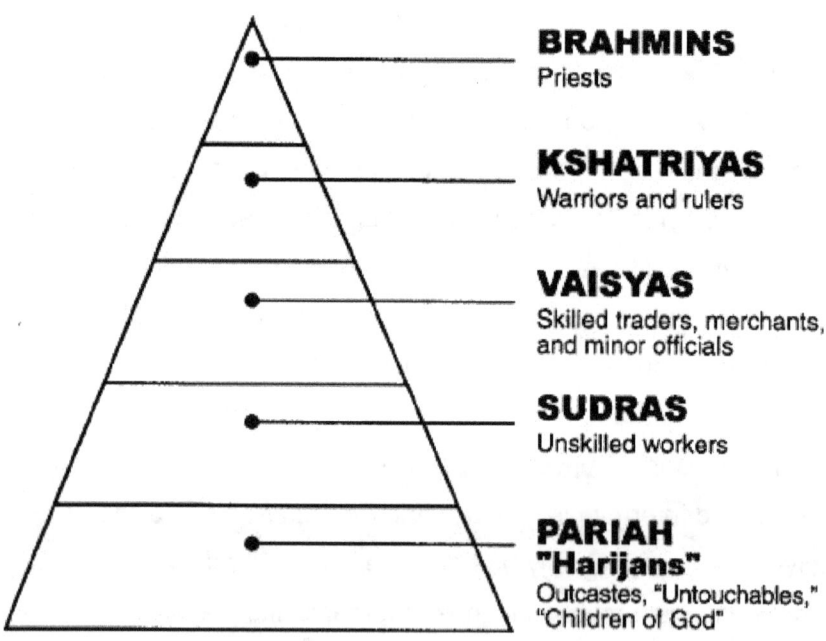

BRAHMINS
Priests

KSHATRIYAS
Warriors and rulers

VAISYAS
Skilled traders, merchants, and minor officials

SUDRAS
Unskilled workers

PARIAH
"Harijans"
Outcastes, "Untouchables," "Children of God"

One of the basic principles of racism is the assignment of people to specific levels of the racial hierarchy in accordance to a social caste system. In the case of U.S. History, the racial caste system was based on skin color that resulted in assigned roles and occupations based on race. The white males were the privileged race and gender, the wealthy and powerful with the right to vote, own land and slaves. They were the Alphas. White women were the Betas whose role was to complement and be obedient to white men. The Gammas were the white merchants and service providers, the Deltas were the indentured immigrant servants and cheap laborers (e.g. Irish and Chinese), and the Epsilon were the black slaves who were sold like cattle.

How has modern society differed in the implementation of a racial caste system? Times have changed greatly in the past 50 years since the passage of the Civil Rights Act and subsequent non-discrimination legislation that affects almost every aspect of society. Yet, while no longer an institutionalized caste system due to the upward mobility provided by capitalism and entrepreneurism, a cursory observation of the race of individuals at each socioeconomic level of society clearly shows a similar pattern of race differentiation not unlike the traditional socioeconomic caste system that is institutionalized in India.

The fact that the United States has an African-American President who was abandoned by his Kenyan father and raised by his Irish mother and Irish grandparents, who lived in Indonesia as a child and was for a time a practicing Muslim before he converted to Christianity (a religious crime punishable by death in some traditional Islamic states), has not changed one bit the stratification of American society primarily as a de facto consequence of race.

President Obama is the token symbolic expression of the non-racism ideal that is promoted by news media and the education system based on the laws on the books.

The largest group of the most powerful and richest people in America continues to be white men, whose white wives receive substantial wealth while married and in divorce. Even though women complain that their average income still falls around 20% below that of the average income for men, if we look objectively at education, years of seniority, and equal performance levels, women are indeed on par with men... as men don't take years off their careers to have babies and to care for them in their early years before returning to the work force. White men continue to be the Alphas, and their women, the Betas. When men of any race become successful, particularly African-American entertainers and athletes, they marry white "trophy" wives to express their conscious and historical subconscious need for social validation. But that still doesn't make them Alphas.

The next level of society are the Gammas... mostly white professionals whether male or female, but increasingly, educated and entrepreneurial individuals from other races who have been able to acquire a modicum level of wealth and political clout through their talents and professions. The Deltas are the recent immigrants, mostly undocumented who provide unskilled labor to fill the manual jobs the Gammas would prefer not to touch. Finally, there are the Epsilons, who are primarily the descendants of African slaves and a more recent phenomenon, Hispanic gangs who are descendants of immigrants. The Epsilon class of society is comprised of the predominantly poor, undereducated, low skilled sector of the impoverished populace who rely on government programs, charity, and crime as their source of subsistence.

Socioeconomic class continues to play a huge role in the upward mobility of individuals and specifically who assigned members choose to associate with in their social networks. Alphas primarily rub elbows with other Alphas, while their Beta spouses become the socialites of high society. The Gammas join professional associations to network their careers and to gain mutual validation of their value to society. The Deltas try to remain anonymous, because being unknown is being un-owned and not deportable. Finally, the Epsilon fill our nation's jails and prisons, that gives Gamma professionals full time employment.

Even though over the past two decades, media has attempted to depict racial minorities in more diverse roles, and less in traditionally stereotypical roles, the reality still exist that stereotypes die hard because sufficient statistics seem to support some aspects of racial stereotypes. For example, blacks tend to be violent, and sure enough they are disproportionately represented in our nation's prisons for the commission of violent crimes. Asians are good at math. Personally, I'm a poor to mediocre mathematician, but my African-American brother-in-law graduated from UCLA with a Masters Degree in mathematics, and he is an exception to the stereotypes, the social generalities based on half-truths and social rules. Racial profiling probably contributed to George Zimmerman (a Hispanic Jew who is classified as a white man) shooting and killing Travon Martin (an African-American teen) because he was afraid this black guy was going to kill him. Stereotypes die slowly and die hard, and too many people needlessly die from it.

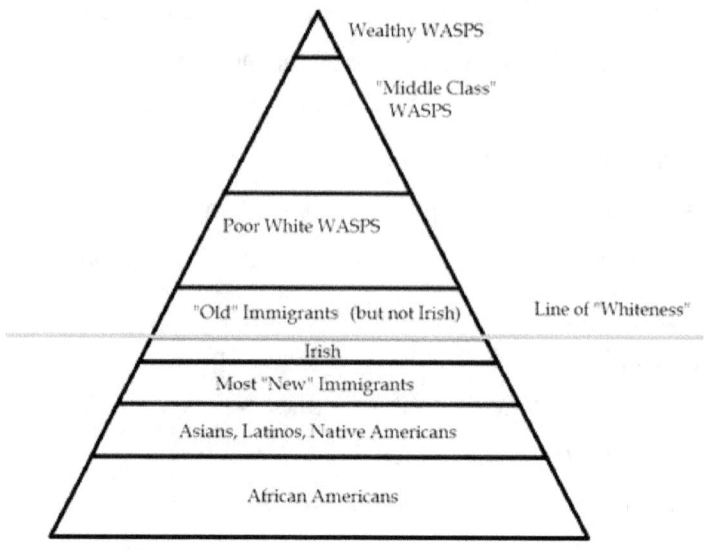

This triangle depicts the hierarchical structure of society around the 1840's to 1850's, when many Irish fled Ireland due to the Potato Famine, and became indentured servants to pay off the cost of passage. Has the socioeconomic strata changed much since the days of slavery? Only the "Line of Whiteness" has moved to include the Irish and most "new European immigrants", and stopped above colored people. During this period, slavery was not yet abolished as the U.S. Civil War was still a decade away, thus Blacks were considered only as 3/5th of a person, and didn't have voting rights.

Other non-white groups faired better than slaves, but they, like the Chinese coolies who helped to build America's first Transcontinental Railroad, were discriminated against and were shunned by the white population. Flash forward to the present time by adding economic levels to this triangle, and we see that the socioeconomic structure of America has not changed much, except the upward mobility of Asians has greatly improved.

Section 4 – Political racism

Speaking of the Zimmerman trial and his acquittal, were Zimmerman an African-American as was Travon Martin, the new media would likely have never picked up this story and woven it into a race issue. Consequently, had President Obama not injected the issue of race into the public arena by stating that if he had a son, he would likely look like Travon, then the issue of racial profiling and racism would probably not have taken hold in the black community. On average Blacks kill 15,000 blacks every year in America, along with 1,600 white and Hispanic people and hundreds of Asians and mixed race people. When blacks kill people from other races, the media and government never interjects the race card. But when a black person is killed by a non-black person or by the police, race and racial profiling is almost always blamed as the mitigating circumstance leading to death. I find that to be incredulous, out of context, and statistically fraudulent... a lie that perpetuates racial disharmony, racial stereotypes, and interracial hatred among the populace.

If Anthropologists are correct, and race doesn't exist biologically or by the known classification methodology that groups all humans into the *Homo sapiens* species, then why does government institutionalize specific racial categories and force them on people at all levels of public programs, including education, census, employment, and other government programs? Consequently, people are encouraged to vote by racial groups to create voting blocks for similar race candidates who share their subcultures and values. A cursory examination of voting records in relation to race clearly show non-whites prefer voting for non-whites

and people of varying races tend to vote for their own race...
specifically, blacks vote for blacks, Hispanics for Hispanics, Asians
for Asians and whites for whites.

When race is not an issue due to the forced choice two-party
option system, voters will cast their votes to reflect their parties,
liberal versus conservative views and the various issues in the
political spectrum. In the absence of a viable white candidate in any
particular party, and a minority candidate appears viable due to
charisma, persuasiveness and popularity, liberal whites have shown
they will vote for non-white candidates. Conservatives and
Republicans continue to pursue their traditional whiteness paradigm
more often than not, and in major elections where there are
sufficient non-white populations, they have lost whenever younger
and liberal whites joined non-whites to vote for viable non-white
candidates, such as Barrack Obama. Even with their failure to
depose Obama in 2012, the GOP still continues their white
exclusivity program.

The bi-partisan comprehensive immigration legislation
passed by the Senate does not appeal to Republican members in
the House because the grass root white voter who live in the "red
states" don't support any non-white agendas proposed by liberal
lawmakers and Obama. The major sticking point is a path to
citizenship for all illegal immigrants currently in the United States.
Republicans object to the inclusion of upwards of 14 million illegal
immigrants eventually becoming citizens because statistics clearly
show minority group voters will usually vote for liberal politicians
who favor government entitlement programs that conservatives feel
are socialistic entitlement programs mostly paid for by white citizens

(whites foot the bill for 85% of welfare programs). Legalizing 12 to14 million illegal Hispanics will only add huge numbers of voters for the Democratic Party. Perhaps, there should be no path to citizenship, but instead permanent residency can be earned by passing specific rational non-race based benchmarks. The Tea Party would be more receptive to that proposal as long as permanent residency does not lead to citizenship.

The government and mass media routinely espouse the mantra that "race shouldn't matter" and Americans of all races possess an equal right to the benefits of the American system. Yet, the government routinely asks for racial identification information through the census and employers. If race shouldn't or doesn't matter, then why create official definitions of various races and ethnic groups, and then make political decisions based upon racial demographics? Why do various politicians court specific racial groups, such as "the black vote", or the "Hispanic vote", or the "conservative white vote" or whatever? This obvious government hypocrisy speaks with a forked tongue through both sides of its mouth.

Political studies one or two decades ago, along with more recent political polls, continue to indicate that the vast majority of Americans neither approve of the jobs their elected officials are doing, nor do they trust their government. After decades of bi-partisan bickering, Americans continue to distrust their government, with only 34% expressing trust in government (McIntosh & Parker, pg.1). Disillusionment with political leaders and dissatisfaction with the way government performs its duties are essential factors that cause distrust of government. However, distrust of government and discontent is not fostering a disregard for the nation's laws, eroding patriotism or discouraging government service, suggesting

Americans are frustrated with government rather than angry with it (M&P, pg.2). Consequently, even though 38% of a small segment who are most angry at government could see justification for violent acts against the federal government (M&P, pg.3), there is no indication that these attitudes are near a crisis stage (M&P, pg.1) to become a threat to our democratic government.

Even during the height of President Clinton's scandalous charges of adultery and perjury, trust declined only modestly (5%) in public opinion polls suggesting that distrust of government is more often connected to how people feel about the overall state of the nation (M&P, pg.1). However, studies also appear to indicate that distrust of political leaders and lack of faith in the political system are principal reasons the public distrust government. It also appears that cynicism about political leaders and the political system is more crucial to distrust than concerns about the proper role of government, worries about its power and intrusiveness, misgivings about its priorities, or resentment about taxes (M&P, pg.5)

Furthermore, the PEW Research Center found in November 1996 that over 60% of survey respondents believed an increase in pessimism about the country's future was due to increasing problems with crime, drugs, and low moral and ethical standards. Perceived level of crime appears to have an opposite correlation on trust, i.e. more murders, less trust (M&P, pg.6). There also appear the potential effects of electoral cynicism and alienation. Academic researchers seek to discover potential causalities in the political culture of our nation to determine the meaning and likely future manifestations of decreasing public trust of our representational democratic system. Does the decline in trust indicate a loss of support for incumbency or for the democratic system? (L&G pg.140). The current level of political trust has steadily declined since 1964 (L&G pg. 137) indicating a steady decline of public trust in government from the 75% level during 1958-64 to recent 20-30% levels, except for the Reagan era when trust rose to the 40% level (F&Z pgs.13,15). The issue of "trust to do right" is described by Klosko (pg. 108) as a concept of perception of legitimacy and personal benefits. Individuals insist on personal interpretations of the same concept (Mason, pg.78), which is evidenced by the tendency of voters to trust the politicians that they elected versus those of the opposing party. In addition Mason (pg. 11) describes the effects of public culture on the perception and expectation of justice as a requisite of trust (Mason, pg. 111).

The relationship between political trust and system stability is thought to be causal by political scientists such as Arthur Miller (L&G pg.140). The decline of trust in government is thought have a potentially negative effect on system stability, however, no empirical evidence lends credence to the view that democratic governance is threatened by floundering trust in the federal government. Are, as Dr. Miller opined, higher levels of distrust for the political system a precursor of "great danger for the American system of government." or is lower trust levels even threatening? (L&G pg. 140).

Analysis of a question posed by National Election Study (NES) interviewers, "How much of the time do you trust the federal government to do right?" attempts to measure the public's attitude toward the democratic system. NES data is cross-tabulated against other variables that may have a causal correlation with this issue, such as social economic status (i.e., SES variables). The federal government referred to in the question is generally agreed to mean the executive and legislative branches.

This paper cross tabulates the question, "How much of the time do you trust the federal government to do right?", using the 1996 NES data base to measure the public's level of trust in government, and whether SES variables differentially modify the reported levels of trust. The hypotheses being tested are that 1) Asian-Americans are more likely to have a higher trust in government than either African-American or white voters; 2) greater trust in government is more likely to occur when respondents feel good about their financial situation; 3) older voters tend to have greater trust in government than younger voters; and, 4) higher levels of information about politics and public affairs leads to increased trust in government. The data results are controlled for gender differences. Political theorists have advanced causal relationships between levels of trust and variables that include levels of knowledge (Mason, pg.107), gender differences (Mason, pg.127), and SES (Parker, pg.446).

Data Analysis

The cross tabulation of 1996 NES appear to suggest certain SES demographic factors are likely to have a direct correlation to a higher or lower than expected level of *trust in government*. Among these hypothesized direct correlates are the following variables:

1. **Race**. Data indicates that Asian-Americans are more likely to have a higher trust in the federal government than African-Americans and whites. A Chisq of (p=0.00) is statistically significant in supporting the data that 44% of Asian-Americans compared to 28% of whites and blacks trust the federal government to do right "just about always" or "most of the time". A tau-b of   -.02 indicates insignificant interaction between dependent variable of trust" and independent variable of "race".

2. **Financial Situation**. A statistically significant probability does not appear to exist according to how respondents viewed their financial situation as a correlate of their level of trust in the government, with approximately 26% to 29% (28.6% average) feeling trust in government "just about always" or "most of the time." A Chisq value of (p=0.01) and a Tau-b value of 0.0 confirm a non-interactive correlation between financial situation and "trust".

3. **Race as Independent Variable, Controlled for Gender**:
    There appears to be a statistically significant difference in the apparent "race" effect for Asian-American males on the question of trust, reporting a Chisq of (p=0.00) and a variance of 6.5% to 9.5% more trust in government "just about always" or "most of the time" when compared to whites

or blacks. A Tau-b of 0.0 indicates virtually no interaction between the variables. In the case of Asian-American females, 52% trusted government in the two top categories stated, as compared to 28.5% to 30.4% for whites and blacks respectively. The results are statistically significant with a Chisq of (p=0.0) and Tau-b of -.04, indicating low interaction between the dependent and independent variables.

Discussion

In addressing the NES question asked respondents, "Do you trust the federal government to do right?", various independent studies suggest correlation between trust and political obligation (Klosko, pg. 8-10), the effects of public culture (Mason, pg. 10), justice (Mason, pg. 11), and fairness (Klosko, pg.128-129). Other political theorists have advanced causal relationships between levels of trust and variables that include understanding of democracy (Mason, pg. 85), expectations (Kimball, pg.715), perception of crime, scandals, and the state of the economy (Chanley, pg.247), alienation and presidential performance (Erber & Lau), and incumbency (Parker, pg.445).

This paper's assessment of NES data does not support a causal relationship between trust and level of knowledge of political information or gender differences. Furthermore, Parker (pg.446) concludes that it is difficult to establish any hypothesized relationship between SES and trust based on previous research due to the ambiguous nature of the findings. For example, some findings indicate that while distrust of government was higher among the lower SES classes, other studies concluded that higher-status groups were more alienated than lower-status groups. Still other studies found no relationship between social class and trust.

Kimball (pg.721) confirmed that participation, income, and political knowledge do not significantly affect the candidacy factor scores, while both partisanship and support for a popular president bears positive effects on congressional approval and trust for government. The cross tabulation of NES data confirms that no statistically significant correlation could be found to link income or political knowledge directly to levels of trust in government.

In the absence of consensus, it is hypothesized that a positive relationship exists between trust in their own elected representatives and socioeconomic status; in other words, each SES group would trust their representatives while distrusted the elected officials of other groups that they do not identify with (Parker, pg.446-7). Parker also expected higher levels of system trust to contribute to higher levels of trust in incumbent representatives, adding that one's own economic plight and government waste are two common economic complaints may contribute to levels of trust in one's elected representative (pg.445).

Only two measures, "race" (Asian-American females) and "age" (R's 65 or over) appear to suggest statistically significant values to the variances from other categories in their data set. In light of the fact that upwards of one-third of Asians and Asian-American females marry outside their race in the U.S., we may surmise that their value for the American people, culture and democracy tends to be generally high, resulting in a higher level of trust for the federal government. In the case of retirees 65 and over, we suggest that their eligibility for government monetary benefits

(Social Security and Medicare) may tend to encourage more favorable attitudes in the federal government, and their regular receipt of monthly checks would certainly tend to favor more trust than distrust. Other potential explanations for the significantly higher level of government trust attributable to both Asian-American females and the elderly may reflect their greater tendency to have "at-home" lifestyles, where issues of crime and violence tend to be less than for the general population who are more interactive in the public and exposed to greater social perils.

Chanley (pg.247) hypothesized that as the proportion of the public who perceive crime as the nation's most important problem rises, trust in government will fall. While Chanley (pg.239-240) stated that while responsibility for changes in government trust levels has been attributed to a variety of causal factors (economic, social-cultural, or political), scholars suggest that trust in government is influenced by the performance of the national economy and citizens' evaluations of the economy, as negative perceptions of the economy promote greater distrust. Second, declining trust has been attributed to social-cultural factors such as rising crime and child poverty. Finally, changes in trust in government have been linked to numerous political factors, including citizens' evaluation of incumbents and institutions, an increasing number of political scandals and increased media focus on political corruption and scandal.

Chanley (pg.239-40) suggest that negative perceptions of the economy (not personal finances), scandals associated with Congress (not information level), and increasing public concern about crime each lead to declining public trust in government consistent with the contention that trust in the federal government is more closely tied to trust in Congress than to the president, they found that allegations of misconduct on the part of Congress exert greater influence on trust in government than do allegations of misconduct by the executive. She concludes that the literature suggests that declining trust in government is a complex phenomenon with multiple potential causes (pg.240).

Parker (pg.442) describes the decline in the influence of political parties as having elevated the importance of voter trust in incumbent public officials. This increased attention is evidenced by elected officials having to spend considerable time encouraging their constituents to "trust them", and that trust in incumbents ultimately influences electoral support for the government. Consequently, Parker (pg.443) believes that a trustworthy legislator, therefore, gains the loyalty of his constituents, stating, "Thus, we believe that trust in a legislator is predicated on the belief that the representative is serving, and will continue to serve, the best interests of his or her supporters rather than acting out of self interest is consistent with a description of constituent trust."

Chanley hypothesized that trust in government is thought to reflect public satisfaction with political leaders and institutions. When presidential and congressional evaluations are favorable, trust in government is expected to increase. Similarly negative evaluations are expected to result in lower levels of trust; however these expectations were not confirmed by their results. Neither presidential nor congressional approval exerts any causal influence on trust... suggesting that presidential and congressional evaluations are as much a consequence of trust in government as they are a cause (pg.251).

Trust may simply boil down to the tendency of people on the losing side in an election to have lower levels of satisfaction with the system than do those on the winning side. Political scientists are interested in attempting
to evaluate the patterns of trust, alienation, and antigovernment sentiment with our democracy is to ascertain the potential threshold at which respect for the system may plummet below "a point of no return." In analyzing the electoral landscape, demographic, attitudinal and political culture are examined and cross-sectioned to determine if there are clear indicants of verifiable predictors of citizens' political behaviors. A cross tabulation of NES (National Election Survey) data from the NES sampling Previous political science research literature and studies have not explained these variances adequately, and any inter-dependencies may be difficult to conclude.

Kimball (pg.722), instead, suggests that citizens appear to make comparisons between what they expect their elected representatives in congress to be like and what they perceive these representatives actually are like, indicating citizens disapprove of congress when they're not getting the congress they want (with honest, community-minded members); or because they feel they're getting a congress they don't want (inhabited by partisan, career-oriented, lawyer legislators).

In our two-party competitive system, the political culture encourages and needs both loyalty and dissent. It is the absence of disruptive acts by a substantial portion of society and not the presence of supportive attitudes that is essential for maintaining an established democracy (F&Z pg. 23-24). Consequently, it is doubtful that distrust of government alone could be a threat to the American system, an opinion supported by Citrin who felt that distrustful individuals were not ready to repudiate the American form of government (L&G pg. 141). Moreover L&G (pg.24) observed that the public perception that "government leaders were corrupt and served primarily special interest groups" contributes to lower trust in government. F&Z (pg.12-13) observed that "...in general, the public has considerable confidence in the institutions of government but not much confidence in the individuals charged with operating these institutions."

Anderson (pg.67) observed that "low levels of citizen support can pose serious problems for democratic systems because both their functioning and maintenance are intimately linked with what and how people think about democratic governance", adding, "... alienation from the issues by both major parties of candidates will lead to declining trust in government we also find evidence that political cynicism is associated with greater approval of anti-government protest...." Prolonged discontent and alienation from the political system many challenge its legitimacy and, ultimately, its very existence. Political participation through the established channels may decrease, and constituents may be tempted to support radical political solutions.

According to Miller, those who disproved of both the Democratic and the Republican policy alternatives in 1968 were the most cynical...Citrin argued that it was dissatisfaction with incumbent leaders rather than their policies that made people cynical. Political scientist study trust in government because (in theory) it reflects on the stability of a country's government. People who distrust their system of government, who do not view it as legitimate are supposedly more prone to antigovernment activities. Research data tend to support this notion of legitimacy, but only as it applies to citizens who display chronic personal feelings about politics.

The basic argument is dissatisfaction with the policy alternatives offered by the two major parties or their leaders causes cynicism, which naturally leads to governmental distrust as evidenced by a greater likelihood to legitimize anti-government feelings and activities. Those who perceive themselves as distant to the issue stands of both the incumbent and the challenging candidate or party will be the most cynical, especially for people with an issues chronicity. They will interpret the trust in government items more in terms of the policies being carried out by those in government and those who disapprove of the ways in which the incumbent handles the job will be most dissatisfied.

A cross tabulation of NES (National Elections Study) data from the year 1996 discloses various correlations between dependent and independent variables, suggesting speculative support of hypotheses that have foundation in previous political science research literature and studies. Explaining the variances and inter-dependencies may be more difficult and conclusions would likely fall short of the criteria for recognition of irrefutable "principles"; however, hypotheses will be ventured as potentially plausible causation of political opinion.

In addressing the NES question asked respondents, "Do you trust the federal government to do right?", the question itself must first be defined in terms of public understanding in respect to popular and political culture. Furthermore, certain factors that contribute to the development of trust or lack thereof should be considered, including political obligation (Klosko, pg. 8-10), the effects of public culture (Mason, pg. 10), justice (Mason, pg. 11), and fairness (Klosko, pg.128-129). Other political theorists have advanced causation relationship between levels of trust and variables that include levels of knowledge (Mason, pg. 107), gender differences (Mason, pg. 127), understanding of democracy (Mason, pg. 85), expectations (Kimball), perception of crime, scandals, and the economy (Chanley), alienation and presidential performance (Erber & Lau), and incumbency (Parker).

A review of the NES data, political and social science theories and culture, the dynamic state of public opinions, and the imperfections of opinion-based research techniques lead me to interpret with caution any statistically significant conclusions that might otherwise be suggested by an analysis of the NES study, or any study based solely on internalized emotionally-based mentations that typify respondents' understanding of, and answers to diversity of interviewers, who by the fact of their gender, appearance, tone, and mannerisms may have affected the honesty level and very nature of the answers received.

The hypotheses tested by cross tabulations of 1996 NES data are:

1. **Race**. It is likely that Asian-Americans have a higher trust in government, and African-Americans feel a lower trust in government than the white electoral majority.

2. **Income Level**. Greater trust in government is likely to occur at the higher income levels.

3. **Educational Level**. Higher educational levels general correlates to a higher level of information about politics and public affairs, and higher economic attainment, which is likely to increase trust in government.

Public perceptions and understanding of apparently simple ideas such as trust, rightness, and governance varies and may be a muddle of presuppositions based upon perceived popular and political culture. Is the concept of "rightness" defined in terms of what voters perceive as a moral value when applied to their judgment of the federal government's actions? The definition of rightness in social and political contexts is situational and relative to each individual's degree of assimilation of the dominant social and cultural values of the majoritarian institutions, including schools, media, religious faiths, and public law. In its daily practice, the perception of rightness is rather a personal edifice based in part upon parental transmission, religious beliefs, and popular culture, with ample rationalization or denial when one's own actions may contradict one's moral opinions and self-image. Consequently, in attempting to explain the NES data set and any variances or lack thereof, the reader should keep in mind the subjectivity of respondents' answers to the question posed by NES interviewers, i.e., "How much of the time do you trust the federal government to do right?" Klosko (pg. 108) discussed the concept of relative rightness and how its perception varied according to perceptions of legitimacy and personal benefits.

Trust is another one of those non-definitive terms that appear to span a gradient in terms of social-political contexts. If an individual were asked if they trust their parents, more likely than not, most people would answer affirmatively. However, that's not to say that any individual would necessary trust their parents with their money, or car, or children, or financial decisions. Yet they could answer emphatically that they in fact trust their parents. The subjectively quantifiable aspects of trust also create a dilemma for data interpretation. How much does a person trust, is like the proverbial, how much does a person love another? Is love and trust absolute concepts, either in theory or practice? I venture to say not.

Finally, "who" or "what" is the federal government? Ask a hundred people and it could mean a dozen different things. After all, the NES interviewers weren't questioning only academicians, who as a group would probably agree somewhat more than the usually disinterested, alienated, apathetic, un-informed or misinformed public, who were the respondents in the study. Is the federal government the executive branch, and if so, do respondents point to the presidency or to the actions of his cabinet, or vice president? Is the federal government also inclusive of the legislative and judicial branches? Is the federal government its bureaucratic agencies, such as the IRS, DEA, CIA, and FBI? Or is the public's concept and definition of the federal government that isolated body of public officials so caught up in mutual and self-aggrandizement that they don't even know there's a world outside of Washington D.C.? Individuals insist on personal and often different interpretations of the same concept (Mason, p.78).

In order to make some sense of the NES data set, the reader should set aside personal definitions of "trust", and "rightness" and "the federal government". The reader should attempt to imagine what the majoritarian's perceived definition of each concept meant when they responded to NES interviewers. Consequently, since there is no effective method to measure or to understand what respondents really meant when they answered the question, "How much of the time do you trust the federal government to do right?"

then let's rely on popular notions of "trust", "rightness", and the "federal government", whatever that might mean to non-political scientists. According to J. Rawls, a political theorist (Mason, pg.10). In addition Mason (pg. 11) describes the effects of public culture on the perception and expectation of justice as a requisite of trust, and further observes the ethics of rights and rightness (Mason, pg. 111) as an interactive contingency between the moral precepts of political culture and the individual's personal self-assessment against those perceived standards. What we can conclude is trust in government is directly reflected by social economic status, including race, income level, educational attainment, social and political privileges or lack of historical human rights. The fact that minority groups in America are substantially less likely to vote, even though the passive of the Voting Rights Act of 1965 forbids voter discrimination on account of race has engendered little added trust in government.

References:

Andersen, Christopher J., and Christine A. Guillory. *Political Institutions and Satisfaction with Democracy: A Cross-National Analysis of Governmental Majoritarian Systems.* The American Political Science Review, Vol. 91, No. 1 (Mar. 1997), pp. 66-81.

Barnes, Samuel H., and Max Kaase. *Political Action.* Beverly Hills, CA: Sage Publications, Inc., 1979.

Brodney, Jeffrey L. *Building Trust in Government.* Journal of Public Administration Research and Theory, Vol. 6, Issue 3 (July 1996), p. 486-491.

Chanley, Virginia A., Rudolph, Thomas A., and Wendy M. Rahn. *The Origins and Consequences of Public Trust in Government: A Time Series Analysis.* Public Opinion Quarterly, Vol 64, (2000), pp. 239-256.

Epstein, Jeffrey H. *American Distrust Their Government.* Futurist, Vol 32, Issue 7 (Oct. 1998), pp. 12-13.

Erber, Ralph, and Richard R. Lau. *Political Cynicism Revisted: An Information-Processing Reconciliation of Policy-Based and Incumbency-Based Interpretations of Changes in Trust in Government.* American Journal of Political Science, Vol 34, No. 1 (Feb. 1990), pp. 236-253.

Harris, Paul. *Civil Disobedience.* Lanham, MD: University Press of America, Inc., 1989.

Kimball, David C., and Samuel C. Patterson. *Living Up to Expectations: Public Attitudes Toward Congress.* The Journal of Politics, Vol 59, No. 3 (Aug. 1997), pp. 701-728.

Klosko, George. *The Principle of Fairness and Political Obligation.* Lanham, MD: Rowman & Littlefield Publishers, Inc., 1992.

Mason, Andrew. *Explaining Political Disagreement.* NY, NY: Cambridge University Press, 1993.

McIntosh, Mary, and Kimberly Parker. *Deconstructing Distrust. How Americans View Government.* Princeton, NJ: The Pew Research Center For The People & The Press, 2001.

Parker, Suzanne L., and Glenn R. Parker. *Why Do We Trust Our Congressman?* The Journal of Politics, Vol. 55, No. 2 (May 1993), pp 442-453.

Section 5 – Poverty and economics

The shifting global power distribution and its effect on ethnicity and race is determined in large part by the effects of capitalism and globalization that has created mega wealth and an elite class of billionaires, whose government minions dictate public policy to people from many nations on all continents. To the elites, race is not their compelling grounds for discrimination in so much as their ownership class separates them from the working classes and the poor. As middle-class income continues to erode from economic stagnation, stock market crashes, recessions, and government monetary policies, the world economic order is less reflective of the traditional hierarchical socioeconomic pyramid and more defined as a bifurcated class construct of the wealthy one percenters versus the rest... a global financially and economically related construction. Who are most likely to express racial prejudice and believe in racial stereotypes? Who are most likely to dislike, discriminate, ridicule, exclude and hate people from other races?

The general formula is rather universal and basic, including the following factors:

- Being wealthy
- Being poor
- Living among impoverished people
- Living in blighted communities
- Enduring repeated violence, particularly when growing up
- Poor education
- Parental and other kinship modeling and pressure
- Peer group validation modeling and pressure

- The social norms from the era of their childhood development

Well-educated people, well traveled people and people with sufficient income and comfortable lifestyles are less likely to be racist. Why? It appears cultural exposure increases tolerance and expands one's perspective on the great diversity that abounds in the world. However, the wealthy elites do make choice on how they personally approach the issue of race. Some avoid dealing with people of other races, but more often than not, "birds of a feather flock together" and the rich hobnob with the rich, celebrities with celebrities, middle-class with those of similar income levels and interests, and the poor are caught in cesspools of generation violence and bigotry due to the harsh subsistence realities that reinforces intolerance as a survival mechanism.

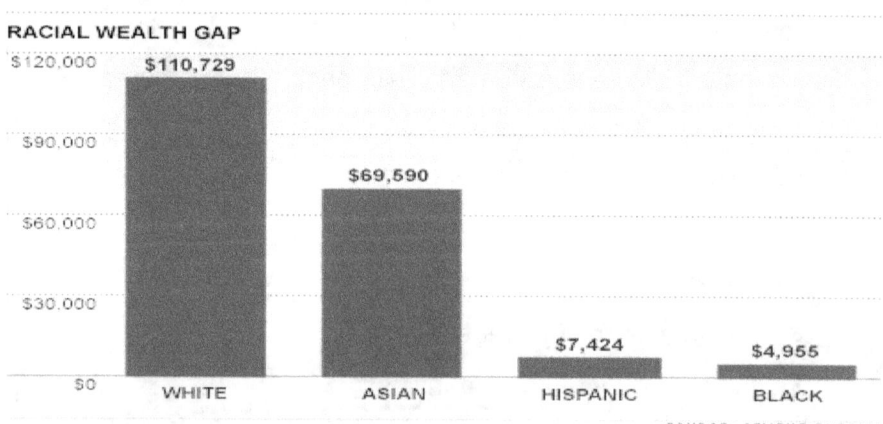

The reality is, a racial wealth gap exists in America, and it has always been there as a pernicious institutionalized system that sets rewards for certain groups to the detriment of others. Were society to be completely "color-blind", then all jobs should be based upon objective measures, and job interviews should be done in a "double-blind" manner, where neither the interviewer or the job applicant sits in the same room and actually sees each other. The criteria for hiring should be based on demonstratable job-related tests and tasks, and not how interviewers may judge applicants' likelihood of

"fitting in" with their corporate culture, based on appearance that naturally includes race. The fact that H.R. managers for most large corporations are white may have some influence on "de facto" discrimination in hiring based on race, though there's not way to prove that without researching their hiring statistics.

Mean net worth by race and ethnicity, excluding the top 1 percent within each race group

	1983	1989	1992	1995	1998	2001	2004	2007	2010
White Non-Hispanic	202,329	284,766	244,362	241,284	307,175	419,235	444,776	488,118	434,480
Black Non-Hispanic	45,866	51,071	57,982	49,409	67,087	73,789	94,409	117,007	74,697
Hispanic	49,703	55,616	59,510	72,718	83,303	75,167	92,773	139,903	69,441
White/Black ratio	4.4	5.6	4.2	4.9	4.6	5.7	4.7	4.2	5.8
White/Hispanic ratio	4.1	5.1	4.1	3.3	3.7	5.6	4.8	3.5	6.3

Source: Authors' tabulations of the 1983, 1989, 1992, 1995, 1998, 2001, 2004, 2007, and 2010 Survey of Consumer Finances (SCF).
Notes: All values are presented in 2010 dollars, and data are weighted using SCF weights.

Mean net worth by race and ethnicity, middle 90 percent within each race group

	1983	1989	1992	1995	1998	2001	2004	2007	2010
White Non-Hispanic	150,306	213,102	181,465	182,674	222,836	295,641	316,495	324,942	296,801
Black Non-Hispanic	34,471	40,708	46,275	39,732	55,932	56,812	70,488	89,348	56,651
Hispanic	42,499	35,518	40,705	55,824	55,040	54,559	68,394	100,651	50,929
White/Black ratio	4.4	5.2	3.9	4.6	4.0	5.2	4.5	3.6	5.2
White/Hispanic ratio	3.5	6.0	4.5	3.3	4.0	5.4	4.6	3.2	5.8

Source: Authors' tabulations of the 1983, 1989, 1992, 1995, 1998, 2001, 2004, 2007, and 2010 Survey of Consumer Finances (SCF).
Notes: All values are presented in 2010 dollars, and data are weighted using SCF weights.

Percentage Change in Share of Income Earned by Each Fifth of U.S. Households: 2010

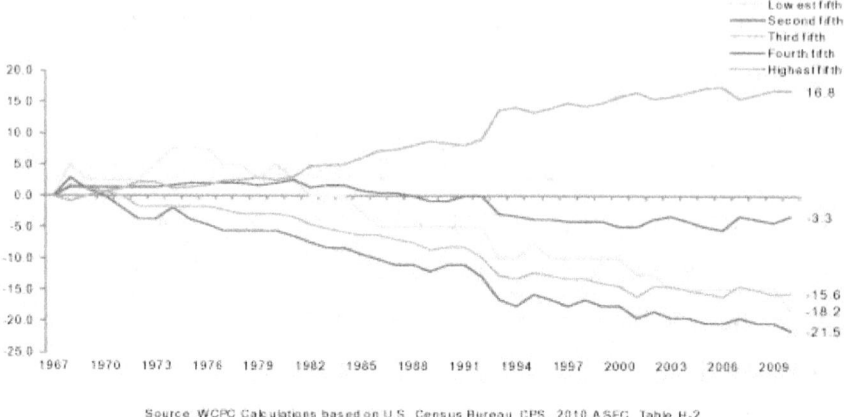

Source: WCPC Calculations based on U.S. Census Bureau CPS, 2010 ASEC, Table H-2

Unfortunately, the solution that is surreptitiously considered and desired by many among the economic elites and powerful is simply to get rid of the problem of poverty and racism by eliminating those who occupy the lowest socioeconomic strata. This idea is commonly referred to by so-called conspiracy theorists as the "Depopulation Agenda" that was first publicly studied by Henry Kissinger, then Secretary of State in 1974, who headed and produced the National Security Study Memorandum 200: Implications of Worldwide Population Growth for U.S. Security and Overseas Interests (NSSM200) that was completed on December 10, 1974 by the United States National Security Council under his direction.

The study concluded that "depopulation should be the highest priority of foreign policy towards the third world, because the US economy will require large and increasing amounts of minerals from abroad, especially from less developed countries," adding, "Whatever may be done to guard against interruptions of supply and to develop domestic alternatives, the U.S. economy will require large and increasing amounts of minerals from abroad, especially from less developed countries. That fact gives the U.S. enhanced interest in the political, economic, and social stability of the supplying countries. Wherever a lessening of population pressures through reduced birth rates can increase the prospects for such stability, population policy becomes relevant to resource supplies and to the economic interests of the United States."

Quotation Source: http://en.wikiquote.org/wiki/Talk:Henry_Kissinger

This policy was adopted as official U.S. policy by President Gerald Ford in November 1975, and was originally classified, but was later declassified and obtained by researchers in the early 1990s. The findings of the report were:

"The basic thesis of the memorandum was that population growth in the least developed countries (LDCs) is a concern to U.S. national security, because it would tend to risk civil unrest and political instability in countries that had a high potential for economic development. The policy gives "paramount importance" to population control measures and the promotion of contraception among 13 populous countries. This is to control rapid population growth which the US deems inimical to the socio-political and economic growth of these countries and to the national interests of the United States, since the "U.S. economy will require large and increasing amounts of minerals from abroad", and these countries can produce destabilizing opposition forces against the United States.

It recommends that US leadership "influence national leaders" and that "improved world-wide support for population-related efforts should be sought through increased emphasis on mass media and other population education and motivation programs by the U.N., USIA, and USAID" in certain named countries:

of which thirteen countries are named in the report as particularly problematic with respect to U.S. security interests: India, Bangladesh, Pakistan, Indonesia, Thailand, the Philippines, Turkey, Nigeria, Egypt, Ethiopia, Mexico, Colombia, and Brazil. These countries are projected to create 47 percent of all world population growth." In addition, this report advocated the "promotion of education and contraception and other population control measures, stating for instance that

'No country has reduced its population growth without resorting to abortion'".

It also raises the question of whether the U.S. should consider preferential allocation of surplus food supplies to states that are deemed constructive in use of population control measures. Some of the key insights of the report were and are controversial, including:

"The U.S. economy will require large and increasing amounts of minerals from abroad, especially from less developed countries [see National Commission on Materials Policy, Towards a National Materials Policy: Basic Data and Issues, April 1972]. That fact gives the U.S. enhanced interest in the political, economic, and social stability of the supplying countries. Wherever a lessening of population pressures through reduced birth rates can increase the prospects for such stability, population policy becomes relevant to resource supplies and to the economic interests of the United States. . . . The location of known reserves of higher grade ores of most minerals favors increasing dependence of all industrialized regions on imports from less developed countries. The real problems of mineral supplies lie, not in basic physical sufficiency, but in the politico-economic issues of access, terms for exploration and exploitation, and division of the benefits among producers, consumers, and host country governments".

"Whether through government action, labor conflicts, sabotage, or civil disturbance, the smooth flow of needed materials will be jeopardized. Although population pressure is obviously not the only factor involved, these types of frustrations are much less likely under conditions of slow or zero population growth".

"Populations with a high proportion of growth. The young people, who are in much higher proportions in many LDCs, are likely to be more volatile, unstable, prone to extremes, alienation and violence than an older population. These young people can more readily be persuaded to attack the legal institutions of the government or real property of the 'establishment,' 'imperialists,' multinational corporations, or other-often foreign-influences blamed for their troubles".

"We must take care that our activities should not give the appearance to the LDCs of an industrialized country policy directed against the LDCs. Caution must be taken that in any approaches in this field we support in the LDCs are ones we can support within this country. "Third World" leaders should be in the forefront and obtain the credit for successful programs. In this context it is important to demonstrate to LDC leaders that such family planning programs have worked and can work within a reasonable period of time."

The report advises, "In these sensitive relations, however, it is important in style as well as substance to avoid the appearance of coercion." Abortion as a geopolitical strategy is mentioned several dozen times in the report with suggestive implications. These are some of the lines:

"No country has reduced its population growth without resorting to abortion."

"...under developing country conditions foresight methods not only are frequently unavailable but often fail because of ignorance, lack of preparation, misuse and non-use. Because of these latter conditions, increasing numbers of women in the developing world have been resorting to abortion..."

Entire quotation downloaded from:
http://en.wikipedia.org/wiki/National_Security_Study_Memorandum_
200

The problem of convincing foreign governments that birth control and abortion were in the national and population interest of Third World nations would have been seen for what it was... a racist driven economic policy to benefit the economic stake holders in the developed world, particularly the U.S. elites. Since a direct approach to depopulate Africa and parts of Asia could never gain global acceptance, and would have likely projected an image of the United States as being a racist holocaust purveyor, so secret efforts were likely made to create a biogenic viral weapon that could be released in Africa... and thus HIV/AIDS was allegedly manufactured in government labs in Fort Detrick, MD, not far from the seat of American federal government and its intelligence infrastructure.

Following is a brief history of the medical research aspect of Ft. Detrick:

November 11, 1969 Veteran's Day.- President Richard M. Nixon requested ratification by the US Senate of the 1925 Geneva Protocol that **prohibited use of chemical and biological weapons**. President Nixon assured Fort Detrick that its research efforts would not be curtailed. (note: Nixon wasn't known for honesty).

November 25, 1969 - President Nixon **outlawed offensive biological research** in the United States. Research at Fort Detrick became focused solely on **defensive measures** – public health considerations, diagnostics, preventive measures, and **treatments for biological warfare infections**. The global telecommunications activities at Fort Detrick remained unchanged.

1971 - President Nixon came to Fort Detrick to announce that he was creating the Frederick Cancer Research Facility of the National Cancer Institute at Fort Detrick. The Department of Health, Education, and Welfare (HEW) (as the Department of Health and Human Services was then) was given title to more approximately 68 acres and 70 buildings in Area A at Fort Detrick.

1972 - The US Army Medical Unit (USAMU) became the US Army Medical Research Institute of Infectious Diseases (USAMRIID) to carry out the research at Fort Detrick under the management of the U.S. Army Medical Research and Development Command (USAMRDC).

1973 -The National Cancer Institute (NCI-Frederick) opened at Fort Detrick on the land and in the buildings to which HEW had taken possession in 1971.

Source: http://www.fortdetrickalliance.org/about/history

Coincidence, or racist conspiracy plot?

How ironic that a decade after President Nixon dedicated a cancer research institute at Fort Detrick, that first signs of the HIV/AIDS epidemic/pandemic first surfaced. "On June 5, 1981, the U.S. Centers for Disease Control and Prevention (CDC) publish a Morbidity and Mortality Weekly Report (MMWR), describing cases of a rare lung infection, Pneumocystis carinii pneumonia (PCP), in five young, previously healthy, gay men in Los Angeles. All the men have other unusual infections as well, indicating that their immune systems are not working; two have already died by the time the report is published. This edition of the MMWR marks the first official reporting of what will become known as the AIDS epidemic.

On June 5, the Associated Press and the Los Angeles Times report on the MMWR. On June 6, the San Francisco Chronicle covers the story. Within days, doctors from across the U.S. flood CDC with reports of similar cases."
Source: http://www.aids.gov/hiv-aids-basics/hiv-aids-101/aids-timeline/

Ask respondents to the NES study on trust in government whether President Nixon was lying when he banned the research on biological warfare weapons, and it's likely a great number of Americans would be skeptical at the least. Now, we have the interesting situation of the deadly Ebola virus that has a mortality rate of about 90% in humans, and due to the infective incubation period and widespread international jet travel in and out of Africa, it is almost certain to spread like HIV/AIDS.

There remains several popular HIV/AIDS origins theories (but of course denied and discredited by the status quo), some of which are summarized in an "in quote" wikipedia article, downloaded without citations from:
http://en.wikipedia.org/wiki/Discredited_HIV/AIDS_origins_theories

"This article contains hypotheses not currently accepted by the majority of the scientific community (note: a majority is 51% or more, so it's possible 49% of scientist may harbor some belief in so-called conspiracy theories based on facts). For the majority view within the scientific community, see History of HIV/AIDS.
Various alternative theories have arisen speculating about the hidden origins of the human immunodeficiency virus (HIV) and the acquired immunodeficiency syndrome (AIDS), ranging from suggestions that they were the inadvertent result of experiments in

the development of vaccines to claims that they were intentionally developed by scientists working for the U.S. government. (Alternative theories regarding the hidden origin—accidental or intentional—of HIV/AIDS must be distinguished from AIDS denialism, which is the view of those who deny that HIV is the cause of AIDS. AIDS denialists, however, overlap with the alternative origin theorists in sharing the conspiratorial view that government officials and the biomedical establishment have been complicit in suppressing the truth about HIV/AIDS.) Speculations notwithstanding, the current scientific consensus is that HIV originated naturally in West Central Africa in the mid-1930s from the closely related simian immunodeficiency virus (SIV)...

Theories:

Smallpox vaccine theory: Purported accidental vaccine origins

In 1987 there was some consideration given to the possibility that the "Aids epidemic may have been triggered by the mass vaccination campaign which eradicated smallpox". An article in The Times suggested this, quoting an unnamed "adviser to WHO" with "I believe the smallpox vaccine theory is the explanation to the explosion of Aids". It is now thought that the smallpox vaccine causes serious complications for people who already have impaired immune systems, and the Times article described the case of a military recruit with "dormant HIV" who died within months of receiving it. But no citation was provided regarding people who did not previously have HIV. (HIV is now considered to be a contraindication for the smallpox vaccine—both for an infected person and their sexual partners and household members.) Some conspiracy theorists propose an expanded hypothesis in which the smallpox vaccine was deliberately 'laced' with HIV.

In contrast, a research article was published in 2010 suggesting that it might have been the actual eradication of smallpox and the subsequent ending of the mass vaccination campaign that contributed to the sudden emergence of HIV, due to the possibility that immunization against smallpox "might play a role in providing an individual with some degree of protection to subsequent HIV infection and/or disease progression". Regardless of the effects of the smallpox vaccine itself, its use in practice in Africa is one of the categories of un-sterile injection that may have contributed to the spread and mutation of the immunodeficiency viruses.

Purported intentional creation

These theories generally attribute HIV's origin to the US government or its contractors. Jakob Segal (1911–1995), a professor at Humboldt University in then-East Germany, proposed that HIV was engineered at a U.S. military laboratory at Fort Detrick, by splicing together two other viruses, Visna and HTLV-1. According to his theory, the new virus, created between 1977 and 1978, was tested on prison inmates who had volunteered for the experiment in exchange for early release. He further suggested that it was through these prisoners that the virus was spread to the population at large. After the end of the cold war, however, the former KGB agents Wassili Nikititsch Mitrochin and Oleg Gordijewski revealed independently of each other that the Fort Detrick hypothesis was a propaganda operation devised by the KGB's First Chief Directorate under the codename "infektion". Later it was also supported by the section X of East Germany's Hauptverwaltung Aufklärung as admitted by its officer Günther Bohnensack. It is not entirely clear whether Segal pursued the hypothesis independently on his own accord or whether he was simply following orders. Segal himself always denied the latter and kept pursuing the hypothesis even after the operation had been canceled and the cold war had ended. It is known that Segal was in close contact with Russian KGB officers and Mitrochin mentioned him as a central asset of the operation.

Various theories have been advanced regarding a "racist" or "genocidal" motivation for the purported creation of HIV. Some theorists also attribute a homophobic element to the conspiracy. These views have sometimes been endorsed by prominent individuals and organizations. In the mid 1980s, the dermatologist Alan Cantwell (see above) included the possibility of a deliberate anti-gay agenda in his theory that the HIV/AIDS epidemic originated with the hepatitis B vaccine in New York City.

In Behold a Pale Horse (1991), radio broadcaster and author Milton William Cooper (1943–2001) proposed that AIDS was the result of a conspiracy to decrease the populations of blacks, Hispanics, and homosexuals. In 2000 South Africa's Minister of Health Manto Tshabalala-Msimang received criticism for distributing the chapter from Cooper's book discussing this theory to senior South African government officials.[18] Nicoli Nattrass, a longtime critic of AIDS denialists, criticized Tshabalala-Msimang for lending legitimacy to Cooper's theories and disseminating them in Africa. The dentist and entrepreneur Leonard G. Horowitz, author of the self-published works Emerging Viruses: AIDS & Ebola. Nature,

Accident or Intentional? (1996) and Death in the Air: Globalism, Terrorism and Toxic Warfare (2001), advanced the theory that the AIDS virus was engineered by such U.S. Government defense contractors as Litton Bionetics for the purposes of bio-warfare and "population control". He believes that HIV was deliberately designed in a US military lab in the 1970s for use as a genocidal weapon.

The Nation of Islam endorses the view that governments and pharmaceutical companies have pursued genocidal racist policies including the creation and spread of HIV. Consequently, the group called for a boycott of U.S.-sponsored vaccination programs for children. Leonard Horowitz has been cited as influential in the NoI boycott decision. In 2008, the controversial Reverend Jeremiah Wright cited Leonard Horowitz in support of his view that the U.S. government invented HIV as a means of genocide against black people.

The 2004 Nobel Peace Prize laureate and environmental activist Wangari Maathai was asked by a Time magazine interviewer if she stood by a previous alleged claim that "AIDS is a biological weapon manufactured by the developed world to wipe out the black race". Maathai responded, "I have no idea who created AIDS and whether it is a biological agent or not. But I do know things like that don't come from the moon. (...) I guess there is some truth that must not be too exposed." Maathai subsequently issued a written statement in December 2004:
"I neither say nor believe that the virus was developed by white people or white powers in order to destroy the African people. Such views are wicked and destructive." (Note: Of course, he likely received professional pressure to retract his prior statements).

Prevalence of conspiracy beliefs

"In 2005, an anonymous survey was conducted among 71 African Americans in the United States to measure belief in prevalent conspiracy theories regarding HIV and AIDS. The survey found that the majority somewhat or strongly believed that "a lot of information about AIDS is being withheld from the public" and over half somewhat or strongly believed that "there is a cure for AIDS, but it is being withheld." Almost 60% disagreed that, "the government is telling the truth about AIDS." Over 40% somewhat or strongly agreed that, "people who take the new medicines for HIV are human guinea pigs for the government." According to Phil Wilson, executive director of the Black AIDS Institute in Los Angeles, conspiracy theories are becoming a barrier to the prevention of AIDS since people start to believe that no matter what the measures they take are, they can still be prone to contracting this disease. This makes them less careful when engaging in practices that put them at risk because they believe there is no point."

While there is little to no evidence that the U.S. government's military lab in Ft. Detrick was responsible for manufacturing the Ebola virus as the "Ebola virus was first isolated in 1976 during outbreaks of Ebola hemorrhagic fever in Zaire and Sudan. The strain of Ebola that broke out in Zaire has one of the highest case fatality rates of any human virus, roughly 90%. Source: http://en.wikipedia.org/wiki/Ebola_virus_disease#History

A Stanford University article stated, "In 1976, Ebola (named after the Ebola River in Zaire) first emerged in Sudan and Zaire. The first outbreak of Ebola (Ebola-Sudan) infected over 284 people, with a mortality rate of 53%. A few months later, the second Ebola virus emerged from Yambuku, Zaire, Ebola-Zaire (EBOZ). EBOZ, with the highest mortality rate of any of the Ebola viruses (88%), infected 318 people. Despite the tremendous effort of experienced and dedicated researchers, Ebola's natural reservoir was never identified. The third strain of Ebola, Ebola Reston (EBOR), was first identified in 1989 when infected monkeys were imported into Reston, Virginia, from Mindanao in the Philippines. Fortunately, the few people who were infected with EBOR (seroconverted) never developed Ebola hemorrhagic fever (EHF). The last known strain of Ebola, Ebola Cote d'Ivoire (EBO-CI) was discovered in 1994 when a female ethologist performing a necropsy on a dead chimpanzee from the Tai Forest, Cote d'Ivoire, accidentally infected herself during the necropsy."

Source: https://web.stanford.edu/group/virus/filo/history.html

After a decade long lull in the advance of the Ebola virus, "An epidemic of the Ebola virus disease (EVD) is ongoing in West Africa. The outbreak is the most severe Ebola virus outbreak yet recorded in regard to the number of human cases and fatalities. The outbreak began in Guinea in December 2013 but was not detected until March 2014, after which it spread to Liberia, Sierra Leone, and Nigeria. A total of 1848 suspected cases with 1013 deaths have been reported by the World Health Organization (WHO) as of 9 August 2014, of which 1176 cases and 660 deaths have been laboratory confirmed to be Ebola."

Bill Gates, Warren Buffet, Ted Turner and other wealthy elitists have become advocates of global depopulation, under the guise of reducing poverty and starvation, reducing population pressure and resultant environmental pollution that are primary causes of species extinction and deforestation, among other justifications. According to an Internet article, entitled, The Billionaire Boys Club: The World's Plutocrats at Work to Decrease Population by Steven W. Mosher that appeared in PRI Review: 2001 (v11, n2) Apr/June, there may be secret agendas behind this call for world depopulation in the Third World. The article is reproduced in entirety, from http://pop.org/content/billionaire-boys-club-worlds-plutocrats-1471

"Who is the biggest funder of anti-people population control programs in the world? If you answered "the U.S. government," you would be wrong. A small group of the world's wealthiest individuals and their foundations collectively fronts more money for the abortion, sterilization and contraception of the human race than Washington. This billionaire boys club includes such plutocrats as Bill Gates (No. I at $63 billion), Warren Buffet (No. 4 at $28 billion), and Ted Turner (No. 25 at $9 billion). These men all have billions on their minds, and not just in their bank accounts. They believe that overpopulation is the greatest threat to the planet, "the single most important issue facing mankind today," brays Ted Turner, founder of the Cable News Network (CNN).

Apparently Turner doesn't read the New York Times, which in its Millennium Edition of 1 January 2000, listed "overpopulation" among the "Myths of the Twentieth Century."[1]

Not only is Thomas Malthus long dead, his "dismal theorem" that growth in human numbers would eventually outrun food supply lies moldering in the grave alongside him. Two hundred years and five billion people later, human beings are living longer, healthier lives than ever before. The "gigantic inevitable famine" that would, Malthus predicted, "with one mighty blow, level . ., the population," continues to recede on the horizon. Every other year humanity sets new records in grain production. Calorie intake continues to climb. Incomes continue to rise, and now average $5,000 a year for every man, woman and child on the planet, up from $100 a year at the time of Malthus.

At the same time, because of longer schooling and other demands of modem life — along with the anti-natal programs of the population controllers — birthrates continue to fall. The bottom line is this: The world's population will never double again. Rather, population will peak around 2040 at 9 billion or so, and then begin to decline. Our long — term problem, in other words, is not going to be too many children, but too few children. Yet the billionaire boys club continues to pour billions of dollars into population control programs to hasten this day. Why? The answer is as varied as the club members themselves.

Ted Turner: Anti-People Zealot

Some may be tempted to dismiss the founder of CNN as a buffoon because of his wild — eyed comments against Christians and babies (he once branded Christianity a religion "for losers" and has advocated a "one-child policy" for the world), but his money and his media influence make him dangerous to ignore. The "Mouth of the South," as he is sometimes called, is currently Vice Chairman of one of the world's largest multimedia conglomerates: AOL Time Warner.

In 1997, for example, the "Mouth" grandiosely announced that he was bestowing $1 billion dollars on the United Nations, making it clear that much of this money would go to population control. To put this figure in perspective, one billion dollars is three times as much as the federal government spends on population control annually.

Turner's cash has gone for such programs as "improv[ing] the reproductive health of adolescent girls in rural Bangladesh" ($1,063,705); Social licensing of reproductive health clinics in Honduras ($2,513,338); and "voluntary confidential counseling and testing for HIV/AIDS, distribution of condoms, treatment of sexually-transmitted diseases, family planning and HIV/AIDS and sexual education" in Mozambique ($2,751,000).

Translated into plain English, this means that Bangladeshi girls as young as ten years old will be given very explicit information about sex, that Honduran girls, both married and unmarried, will be encouraged to contracept and (in case of contraceptive failure) to abort, and young men and women in Mozambique will have their cultural and religious traditions trashed by the blatant promotion of both homosexuality and unmarried sexual activity. All of which in turn drives down the birth rate.

The closest Turner has come to his dream of a mandatory population control policy is bankrolling efforts to reduce the number of children born to refugees. His UN Foundation recently gave $5.9

million to the United Nations Population Fund (UNFPA) and the United Nations High Commissioner for Refugees (UNHCR) "to develop and distribute emergency reproductive health information and services to refugees in emergency situations" in Central Asia and several regions in Africa.

Our investigations at PRI have revealed that the "emergency reproductive health information and services" include so-called morning after pills and manual vacuum aspirators, both of which are used to perform early-term abortions.

During the recent crisis in the Balkans, Turner's UN Foundation was even more explicit about its anti-natal aims. One award given to the UNFPA was for, in the foundation's words, "emergency work in the Kosovo region, where about 10 percent of the 743,000 refugees are either pregnant women or newborns, and 1000–1500 births a month are expected among the refugees." In the view of the Ted Turners of the world, refugees shouldn't have any babies.

Not surprisingly, Turner's misanthropic views have found their way into CNN's programming. "Captain Planet and the Planeteers" was an environmentally correct cartoon character who did battle with notorious polluters around the world, including … families with more than two children. One early assault was entitled "Population Bomb." But the series reached an all-time low with "Numbers Game," in which two of Captain Planet's "planeteers" get married and begin "irresponsibly" having children. Soon they "feel like the old woman in the shoe, with a dozen hungry children, and another one in the oven." The earth itself (called "Gaia" in the New Age parlance of the series) whispers to the repentant couple that the ideal family has only one or two children. Larger families only lead to hunger, poverty, and pollution.

Turner recently made his most chilling proposal yet. Speaking to the pro-abortion group, Zero Population Growth, he called for the forceful implementation of a worldwide policy of limiting every couple to one child. The idea for a "one-couple, one-child" policy is not original with Turner, of course. For the past twenty years the Chinese Communist Party has been busily pursuing their own version. The Chinese people, who have been aborted and sterilized by the tens of millions, might be able to tell Turner a thing or two about how "forceful implementation" of a one-child policy works in practice.

But it is unlikely that Turner would listen. For he believes, right down to his secular humanistic core (he was once honored as "Humanist of the Year" by the American Humanist Association), that he is saving humanity from itself by preventing it from reproducing. The banner quote on the Turner Foundation website reads "I see the whole field of environmentalism and population as nothing more than the survival of the human species."

Turner is a strange, unpredictable man in many ways, but on the issue of population he is an open book. The world's troubles, he typically remarked at a recent speech at the University of Idaho, stem from the too — rapid growth of the human race. When he was born in 1938, the world population was about 2 billion. It recently reached 6 billion, he said, while the white rhino population has dropped by 99 percent over the same period. "The more of us there are, and the more stuff we use, the more impact we have," he said.

And the more people there are to watch CNN, and read TIME magazine, and watch Warner Brothers movies, one might add, activities that white rhinos rarely engage in.

Warren Buffet: No Project Too Controversial

Warren Buffet's business accomplishments are impressive enough. Beginning with an antiquated New England textile mill, the billionaire septuagenarian has built Berkshire-Hathaway, Inc., into a publicly traded monolith that is the majority shareholder in Coca-Cola, Dairy Queen and numerous other companies ranging from newspapers to candies. And Buffet, both Chairman of the Board and majority shareholder of Berkshire-Hathaway, has been careful to maintain absolute control as his investment vehicle picked up speed. It is no wonder that "the Oracle of Omaha" is idolized by Wall Street as a financial genius.

Unlike Turner, who throws around money and opinions like a pinwheel, Warren Buffet is notoriously tight-lipped and tight-fisted. Reportedly, he once denied a loan to his own daughter. And he has never said much about his philanthropy. His foundation, meager compared to that of other billionaires at $22 million, must be judged on what it does. And what it does, mostly, is hard-edged, even fanatical, population control.

The Buffet Foundation is known for funding projects that other foundations, even those similarly inclined to limit human numbers, keep well clear of, such as the deadly abortion drug, RU-486. Back in 1994 Buffet provided $2 million to the chief US promoter of the drug, the Population Council, key funding that was used to fund the clinical trials of RU-486 that led to its later legalization by the Food and Drug Administration (FDA).2

Another $2 million went to North Carolina's Family Health International (FHI) for an equally questionable drug, quinacrine hydrochloride. Originally developed as an anti-malarial drug, quinacrine has in recent years been used to perform chemical sterilizations on women. Inserted into the upper part of the uterus, the quinacrine hydrochloride tablets dissolve to form a powerful acid which burns away the lining of the upper uterus and fallopian tubes. The resulting scarring usually renders a woman sterile. If her fallopian tubes are not completely blocked, any babies she subsequently conceives cannot implant.

Family Health International (FHI) initiated testing of quinacrine as a sterilization agent as early as 1976, But its 1981 application to the FDA to approve the drug for sterilizations (it had previously been approved to treat malaria) was rejected on the grounds that, as FHI later explained, "rigorous studies are needed to ensure the safety and efficacy of quinacrine."3 Buffet's fresh infusion of cash will apparently jump start this process by enabling the testing to go forward.

In the meantime, ignoring the FDA's ban on the use of the drug in the United States, quinacrine's proponents are doing a brisk business overseas. The Vietnamese government has sterilized tens of thousands of poor women using this method, many without their foreknowledge or consent. Recent reports suggest that ethic minorities, such as the Hmong and Montagnard, are being specifically targeted. Although quinacrine sterilizations have been banned in India, New Delhi newspapers report that more than 30,000 impoverished, illiterate women have been subjected to the painful procedure. Informed consent is often lacking, and follow up care is nonexistent.

Buffet's favorite charity, at least to judge by his giving, is an obscure entity with the studiously neutral name of International Projects Assistance Services (IPAS). According to a Business Week report, the foundation's "1999 contribution of $2.5 million is part of a five-year, $20 million commitment, which will enable IPAS to double its capacity." Double its capacity in what? Aborting very small babies up to twelve weeks of age by means of a hand-held suction pump, that's what. As it turns out, IPAS is the principal manufacturer and distributor of the manual vacuum aspirators, or MVAs, used by the UN Population Fund, and other groups. This deadly device is actually a manually operated suction pump that can be used perform, in IPAS words, "elective abortion through the first trimester." When the tip is inserted into the uterus, and the operator pulls the plunger on the 50cc syringe, enough vacuum is created at the tip to suck a tiny baby right out of her mother's womb.4

Nor is IPAS's abortion advocacy an anomaly. A list of Buffet's charitable contributions read like a veritable rogue's gallery of abortion promoters and providers. Such groups as the National Abortion Rights Action League (NARAL), the Center for Reproductive Law and Policy, and Pathfinder International figure prominently. And in a particularly nasty twist, his funding to Planned Parenthood is specifically earmarked to enable particular clinics around the country to perform abortions.5

What would possess a man of obvious intelligence and untold wealth to spend tens of millions of dollars to finance aggressive programs of sterilization and abortion? To put it even more bluntly, why is Warren Buffet obsessed with ridding the globe of "excess" baby humans? Unlike Turner, Buffet doesn't bare his soul every time he opens his mouth. Yet the two may have more in common than it appears. His biographer, Roger Lowenstein, reports that Buffet has "a Malthusian dread that overpopulation (will) aggravate problems in all other areas — such as food, housing, even human survival." And like Turner, Buffet not only rejected, but developed a strong antipathy to, his parent's Christianity.

So Buffet lounges in his office in Omaha, sipping Cherry Cokes and plotting billion-dollar investment strategies, while thousands of poor Indian women are being scarred for life with quinacrine, or having their babies sucked out of their wombs by manual vacuum aspirators that he has helped provide. It is sad that this Midas-like character, so blessed with material goods, should take so misanthropic a view of the people with whom he shares the planet, and from whose existence he profits. Even if he doesn't recognize the Indian as a fellow creature of God, surely he knows that they are tremendous consumers of Coke.

Bill Gates: Billionaire in Conflict?

The youngest member of the Billionaire Boys Club at 44 — and also by far the wealthiest — Bill Gates would not appear to have much in common with the other two, either personally or professionally. Unlike Ted Turner, who was diagnosed a manic-depressive in the eighties and is separated from Jane Fonda, his second wife, Bill Gates seems pretty normal for the world's most famous computer nerd. He is, by all accounts, happily married to Melinda French Gates, who is a practicing Catholic. And the pre-nuptial1 agreement that Melinda had Bill sign calls for their children (they presently have two) to be raised in the Faith.

Unlike Warren Buffet, a stock market speculator who has parlayed price earnings ratios into vast wealth, Gates is a world-class entrepreneur who has built a multinational company from the ground up. Not the kind of person, one would imagine, to become fixated on numbers, human or otherwise, or to fall back on simplistic Malthusian arguments. And he has poured billions (to Buffet's millions) into his foundation.

But Gates appears to be of two minds when it comes to population growth. Gates the Entrepreneur believes, as he said in a 1996 interview with Forbes magazine, that "Julian Simon [population growth advocate] is right and Paul Ehrlich [population doomsayer] is wrong... I think the world is progressing... Resources are becoming more abundant. I'd rather go into a grocery store today than to a king's banquet a hundred years ago."6

Just three years after this ringing endorsement of human progress, however, the associate director of William P. Gates Foundation was claiming that her Chairman held much more pessimistic views: "Bill Gates ... has a very legitimate concern over the burgeoning population of the world. Within the month the population of the world will reach 6,000,000,000 people, with nearly two-thirds of them malnourished, uneducated, and lacking the skills and training necessary to cope with their lives."7

Will the real Bill Gates please stand up?

It is hard to believe that Gates the Entrepreneur would lose any sleep over the prospect of six billion customers. Nor would he casually dismiss four billion Africans, Asians, and Latin Americans two-thirds of humanity — as "malnourished, uneducated, and lacking the skills and training necessary to cope with their lives." That would be as disrespectful as it is dishonest: The claim that "two-thirds of the world's population is malnourished" was invented by the United Nations back in 1950. It was false then, and it is even more out of step with reality today.8

The claim that these peoples are "'uneducated'" is simply untrue. Over 80% of the world's population is literate, according to UN statistics.9 The claim that these peoples can't "cope with their lives" is beneath comment, but their "skills and training" are matters of public record. According to UN statistics, over 70% of children in India and over 95% of children in China attend primary and secondary schools.10 The same kind of doom and gloom that Gates the Entrepreneur once sought to dispel is now, in a strange twist of fortune, being advocated — and funded — by the Gates Foundation.

The German Foundation for World Population (Deutsche Stiftung Weltbevolkerung) received a $545,000 grant to help bring about "a humane decline in world population growth."11 Population Communications International also benefited from a grant, and went on to produce a video called "Jam Packed," a pessimistic commentary on world population. Gates may like American grocery stores but in "Jam Packed" they are a symbol of American decadence.12

The International Planned Parenthood Federation (IPPF) affiliate in the Dominican Republic, PROFAMILIA, has received Gates funding, Cardinal Nicolas Lopez Rodriguez, the Archbishop of Santo Domingo, recently compared PROFAMILIA's sterilization campaign against local women to the work of "death squads."

The Peruvian Institute of Responsible Fatherhood, INPARRES for short, has received a grant. The organization, another IPPF affiliate, has collaborated with the Peruvian government's coercive sterilization campaign, in which women were sterilized in unhygienic conditions under a quota system. Tanzania's state family planning organization, UMATI, has also received funding from the Gates Foundation. Tanzanian women complain that UMATI routinely violates human rights, injecting contraceptives such as Depo-Provera and Norplant without informed consent, and has performed forced abortions and sterilizations.

Still, Gates the Entrepreneur may be making a comeback. He and his wife have recently announced that the Gates Foundation will put up $750 million to establish the Global Fund for Children's Vaccines. Their goal is to immunize every child in the world against diphtheria, measles, polio, tetanus, tuberculosis and whooping cough. If they are successful, they will save one and a half million children each year from these deadly but vaccine-preventable diseases. And in years to come these diseases, like smallpox, will exist only in memory.

Which Bill Gates will ultimately prevail? Will it be Gates the Entrepreneur who sees man, with his God-given intelligence, as the ultimate resource? Or will it be Gates the Doomsayer who sees further growth in human numbers producing only misery? There is a lot riding on his decision. About 70 billion dollars, in fact."

Endnotes:

1 New York Times, 1 January 2000.

2 "The Buffett Foundation has helped finance research on the abortion pill. RU-486," http://www.fas.harvard.edu/~jtownsen/zpg-boston/turner.html.

3 Report in Celebrate Life, originally from the Omaha World Herald.

4 http://www.ipas.org/ipas/mva/index.html.

5 http://www.plannedparenthood.org/abortion/Default.htm. Buffett money has enabled dozens of Planned Parenthood clinics to add abortion services.

6 http://www.forbes.com/asap/120296/html/bill%5Fgates.htm, Forbes magazine, 12/2/96, see also http://www.fumento.com/simon.html.

7 September 13, 1999 letter from Gates Foundation to American Life League, http://www.billgateseducate.com/steps06.htm.

8 The Ultimate Resource, Julian L. Simon, 1996, p. 95–94, http://www.inform.umd.edu/EdRes/Colleges/BMGT/.Faculty/JSimon/Ultimate_Resource/TCHAR05.txt.

9 http://dailynews.yahoo.com/h/ap/19991011/us/day_of_6_billion_1.html, Associated Press news story, 10/11/99.

10 World Statistics Pocketbook, http://www.un.org/Depts/unsd/, United Nations.

11 http://www.dsw-online.de/objectives.html, German Foundation web site.

12 http://www.gatesfoundation.org/pressroom/release.asp?PRindex=55, Gates Foundation web site; **http://www.population.org/resource.htm**.

Section 6 – Reverse racism

The Holocaust killed almost 6 million Jews and 2 million gypsies, mentally ill, retarded, homosexuals and other people Hitler and his Nazis felt were inferior or degenerate in his attempt to "purify" the Germanic/Aryan race in Europe. Does the fact that these groups were victimized give their descendants the right, or entitle them to persecute others if they feel they might be targeted for hatred or discrimination? Does the history of slavery endured by African-Americans make their descendants victims of slavery, even though slavery has been outlawed for centuries and there isn't a black person alive who has personally been held as a slave in America. Subsequent to the abolishment of slavery pursuant to the U.S. Civil War, racial discrimination and "de facto" segregation persisted in many parts of America and African-Americans resorted to civil disobedience to gain the support of the federal government to abolish racial discrimination.

With the abolishment of slavery and outlawing of institutionalized racial discrimination and segregation, there isn't a person alive today who can be legally subjected to these inhumane practices. However, there is a phenomenon in society that appears to give an exemption to charges of bigotry and racism to blacks while exaggerating those claims against whites. In addition, individuals from minority groups who express racial hatred, prejudice and racist behaviors appear to be given a pass when directed at each other or against whites. Does that mean colored people are incapable of racism, and the legal system only applies racial discrimination statutes against whites? This appears to be true as a significant percentage of people from racial minority groups exhibit ignorant and overt demonstrations of racism, usually as part of their subcultures.

"Reverse racism" and other fables.

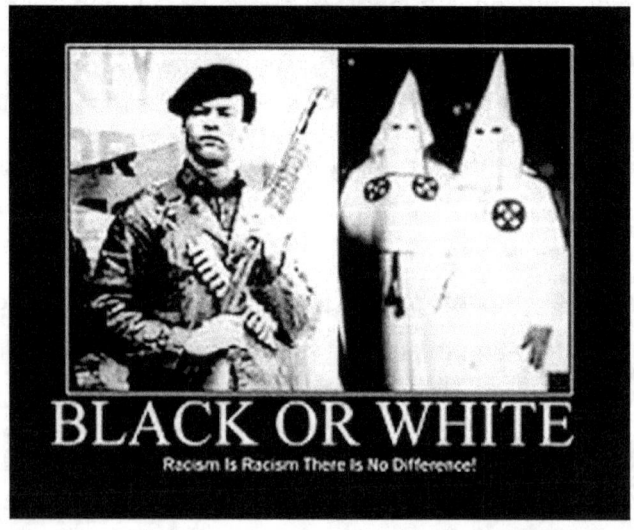

Section 7 – Racial determinism

In the American political and legal system, there are unalienable rights that are guaranteed by the Bill of Rights in the U.S. Constitution, among which are the freedom of speech, freedom of the press and freedom of association... freedom of choice. However, in the practice of these supposed freedoms, restrictions are placed upon the populace to limit their expression. For example,

- Freedom of speech – fully one-third or more of Internet bloggers and commenters engage in hateful speech, name calling, insults and threats rather than simply to state their opinions. Teachers can not state their personal beliefs while teaching in the classroom, but only make statements that reflect the educational curriculum, or be subject to administrative actions up to and including forced resignation. Only tenured professors have a modicum degree of "academic freedom" to publish their opinions, and where their writings are found to be offensive to their employing university, its faculty or administrators, they can be censored and steps taken to terminate their employment. Don't use certain words while on board commercial airlines... just uttering the words bomb, gun, hijack or other inflammatory words and phrases subjects the speaker to detention or imprisonment. Get the idea? Politically correct speech is welcomed, but all other opinions carry potential penalties. So much for free speech... another conditional illusion and not a right.

- Freedom of the press – how many journalists have been jailed for their unwillingness to disclose their confidential sources to the government? If a journalist is called to testify before Congress, could they muzzle their response and cite freedom of the press – or must they rely on taking the 5th Amendment to avoid recrimination? Neither can be effective because any journalist, or anyone, can be held in contempt of Congress and jailed indefinitely until they cooperate. So much for freedom of the press. Of course politically correct, sensationalistic, scandalous and celebrity gossip press sells, so that's okay. But a disclosure of the inner workings of the NSA will surely brand one a traitor, and his supporters as accomplices who aids and abets traitors like Edward Snowden and obstruct justice by harboring him. Even with the international drag net out for Snowden for making public confidential government files and the help of another leaker and whistleblower, Julian Assange of Wikileaks, Snowden has become a man without a country, subject to arrests or possible assassination.

- Freedom of association. Not if the government has anything to do with it. Any public or private institution, company or agency who receives government funding, or whose clients receives government funds that are paid for services from such entities is not free to choose their associations based on protected classes such as race, sex, disability, religion, age and soon, sexual-preference. So if you are a white red neck who wants to keep your children exposed only to other white red necks and Aryan supremacists, the government won't permit you to do so if they've decided your child should be bussed to a predominantly black school to create a racial balance. Where in the U.S. Constitution does it state that a racial balance is a government right of mandate? It doesn't, but the courts have twisted legalese to justify anything they want.

- In conclusion, we value pedigree dogs and have a national association to set standards for each breed, but how hypocritical that we won't allow human beings the freedom of choice to decide who they wish to associate with. If we mix all of the races in America, it will soon become a nation of mutts, hybridized individuals without sense of where they came from, of a lost of tradition, identity and heritage. We worry about the rapid lost of biodiversity in nature, and artificial preserves are created to protect the purity of their endangered species. White reproduction rate is by far below that of the non-white population, even with China's one-child policy. If we encourage and force race mixing and its probable consequences (don't forget white slave owners often had bastard children with their slaves), then we llmit freedom of association and threaten the continued existence of distinct racial and ethnic groups that left alone without government intervention and mandates, appear totally happy associating with people like themselves who share similar subcultures, values and race.

Section 8 – Racial persecution

Voluntary racial segregation is a reality reserved to non-white people. Mexicans usually live among other Mexicans in communities such as East L.A., as Asians tend to live among other Asians in communities such as Monterey Park, while South L.A. comprises black communities, whites live in Canyon Country or Malibu and Iranian Jews live in Beverly Hills. However, should a non-white be able to afford Malibu, there are laws that force white neighbors to accept the residence of non-white homeowners. Where there exist an undercurrent of friction between blacks and Hispanics, there have been episodes where Hispanic gang members have torched homes of blacks who moved into their territories. These are social reactions based on racism, or excluding other races.

There is a difference between voluntary racial association (or for that matter, religious, sexual preference, cultural, etc.) and forced racial discrimination. Voluntary segregation is freedom of association. So if a white family wished to join a white Supremacist group that excludes non-whites, they should be able to do so without government sanctions. Other racial groups do that all the time, and it never becomes a public policy issue when for instance Chinese choose to live among other Chinese in Chinatown and join Chinese family associations. Where adverse discrimination comes in is when, for example, a white family wants to move to Chinatown (which is highly unlikely, for as an illustrative example), and the Chinese neighbors block them from buying a house in Chinatown due to racial discrimination. On the flip side, a Chinese family should be allowed to buy a home in an all white neighborhood if they can afford it, and the white neighbors have a right to exclude the Chinese family from their social association, but don't have a right to keep them from buying the house, or to use any form of intimidation, violence or social harassment to "get 'em outta Dodge."

Ex-U.S. Ambassador to China, Gary Locke and his family

Section 9 – Changing attitudes

The Republicans are back on their heels from its failure to gain a majority in the Senate and inability to elect a GOP President to replace Obama. Political pundits have determined that the shifting political spectrum reflecting greater participation in the voting process by a higher number of racial minorities has tipped the scale toward liberalism versus conservatism. The ultra right wing of the GOP reflecting conservative small town views held by relatively homogenous white Americans stands in marked contrast to the liberal leanings of city folks whose exposure to interracial cooperation in the work place is commonplace for all racial groups, whites, blacks, brown, yellow, red and mixed races.

The primary reason the Tea Party and most GOP politicians are against comprehensive immigration reform that provides a path to citizenship is it permits upwards of 14 million illegal immigrants, of whom over 95% are non-white (not including those lighter skin Hispanics who may otherwise consider themselves white) and more likely to vote for liberal candidates and those from minority groups than for white people. Even were Obama to take the path to citizenship out of the bipartisan Senate compromise bill and instead replace citizenship with an orderly path to obtaining a "green care" or permanent residency without the possibility of citizenship, the House conservatives pressured by Tea Party activists would most likely block that attempt also because it would give the natural born children of green card holders automatic birthright citizenship. It would be possible as a voting block for the natural born citizen children of permanent residents to push for future changes to enfranchise their parents.

Chapter 2 - Global racial inequities

Since 1950, domestic events have occurred during tumultuous times amidst astounding scientific and technological advances, for better and for worse. We've witnessed via the media, volumes of photographs, videos, and reports of human atrocities against humans. I'm thankful that I was spared WW2, the A-bomb, and internment camps, but the decades of violence that followed were in many ways equally abhorrent, if not more so. The civil rights era, the Vietnam War, assassinations of JFK, MLK, RFK, MalcomX, Ghandi, and many lesser known patriots and humanitarians set the stage for contemporary state and non-state acts of violence.

The horrific inhumanity of the Jewish Holocaust was only a few decades later followed by Pol Pot's Khmer Rouge slaughter of perhaps 8 million Cambodians. Ide Amin was known to laugh out loud when slaughtering hundreds of thousands of his own people in Uganda, the Tutus and Hutus in Rwandans kill each other still, and China had witnessed the executions, imprisonment, and torture of millions. It has not been a peaceful world, as technology has both advanced the efficiency and effectiveness of violence, while acting as a partial deterrent in the international arena.

We may wondered silently why these atrocities were allowed to continue over the years by the Western political/military elites, who typically foster grand sounding humanitarian ideals, yet whose actions have often proven to betray those principles they pretend to espouse. Isn't the life of an African, or Asian, or Jew equally worth that of a Briton, American, German, or Swede? I surmise from standard of living statistics, that in the scales of the First World Hegemon, the answer is an emphatic "No." Therein lies the basis of the international struggle between peoples, races, and ethnic groups. Our own American history provides a prime example of First World tactics, when the genocide of Native Americans followed a pattern of false promises, broken treaties, and military violence.

What does the First World Hegemon want that entails tolerance of inhumanity in non-white states and support of oppressive juntas in third world nations, which it attempts to prevent in Europe? The historical colonialist mentality still runs strongly through the blood lines of Europe's elites; only the revisionist strategy for world domination no longer lies in direct military confrontation, but in global economic control and domination, juxtaposed by military intimidation. Their vision continues to be one of a united Europe as the center of civilization, a feat first attempted by European royalty, and now made possible by the creation of multi-national corporate conglomerates owned by Europe's elites. What they weren't able to accomplish with real people, they now are accomplishing through fictional entities (legal immortal corporations) and the utilization of technology.

Europe is in fact no more than a fictional continent created to satisfy an egomaniacal self-aggrandizing need to overcompensate for early European backwardness and warring heritages. Europe is not physically a continent, but merely the western end of the Asian continent. This drive to create fictional entities (corporations), fictional (and worthless) monetary systems, deceptive and untruthful marketing, political, and bureaucratic institutions and ideals are all part of their larger scheme of world domination. The First World Anglo-Germanic European-American plan for world domination is essentially the same in principle as it was when "The sun never set on the British Empire", only the methods have been disguised and repackaged to appear beneficial to the peace and economic development of the developing world. It's a sales pitch that is likely to result in Third World genocide.

The smoke screen for the new world order is the accelerating dependency of developing world markets on the Western monetary system, the creation of a future justification for military intervention to protect Western assets, and the future wholesale rape of third world resources as repayment to World Bank members. The gradual genocide of Third World peoples through poverty, disease, racism, class warfare, violence, and military interventions (conventional, genetic, and nuclear) are the future methods of genocide. At the rate AIDS is decimating the population in Sub-Saharan Africa, NATO and UN troops, backed by First World corporate interests, will be called on in the future to "stabilize" Africa's infrastructure, as a pretext to develop its vast stores of natural resources for western products and consumption. The "silk road" to the eventual rape of Africa will be carved by bulldozers and the tracks of military vehicles.

Few politicians or academicians will publicly admit or profess to discern the reality that stares down humanity today, and the likely outcomes of global political-economic policies dictated by the First World bloc of nations that comprises the white race. Their methods of self-propagation are many, including technological advantage, genetic weapons, economic destabilization, cultural imperialism, and first strike nuclear projection. Is it their goal to eventually limit world population to 2 billion humans, comprised of 1 billion whites (Alphas), and 1 billion colored races (Betas)? Is their hidden agenda to rid the world of the poor, illiterate, disabled, retarded, and non-elites over 50 that comprises over 80 percent of the planet's colored races?

Applying a global market economy paradigm, the Betas would serve the Alphas by producing goods and services from industries owned by the Alphas. According to Marxist theory, the Alphas would own the means of production, and the Betas would supply the labor. The Alphas (boursequoise elites) would obtain the best, with the lesser grade products available to the Betas (workers class). This "ideal" configuration will save the planetary environment by eliminating pollution from developing nations, massive waste products of human consumption, and the depletion of natural resources by an exploding world population (projected to reach 30-50 billion by 2100, if supportable by earth). The world would become relatively stable because the white hegemony of so-called democratic states will be able to manage world resources according to the WTO & World Bank "standards." Developing nations, weakened by AIDS and diseases from GM (genetically modified) foods, will depend on the West to assist them, which will instead present a Trojan horse, the appearance of benign humanitarian aid, laced with genetic disease, political corruption, and economic dependency.

I.   The First World Hegemon's Anti-Third-World Genocide Strategy

A.   Economic dominance by the World Bank; dependency of developing nations' economies under the threat of monetary destabilization. The west is waiting for AIDS to decimate and weaken African and Asian governments to the point they may step in to "restore order and for humanitarian reasons", install corrupt puppet governments, and then export the natural resources of those continents while enslaving their peoples to supply cheap labor for products of western consumption.

B.   Cultural imperialism via the Internet, music, movies, clothing, food, and other deceptive marketing ploys to "sanitize" the world of non-western ideas, customs, cultures, and religions that do not conform to the ideal profit making motive of the globalized market system.

C.   Political colonialism via infectious spread of "scientific management" and other western legal and bureaucratic concepts, and through bribery and corruption of developing world governmental elites through the use of food and medicines as coercive strategies.

D.   Military domination by embargo of developing nuclear states, supporting destabilization of non-cooperative states, projecting secret genetic and viral warfare materials into the Third World (e.g., AIDS, genetically modified foods), developing a nuclear missile shield, and targeting nukes at developing Third World nations as future nuclear extortion.

The projection of First World nuclear and economic power against the Third World are parts of a secretly formulated strategy to give world dominance and control to Euro-America. History and contemporary events indicate that there exist a real (secret), though subtle conspiracy among the Anglo-Germanic elites (and their white American descendants) who control world resources to maintain their superior position through policies that directly or indirectly result in the genocide of the world's non-whites.

References:

Christopher Keith Hall. "The First Five Sessions of the UN Preparatory Commission for the International Criminal Court (in Current Developments)." *American Journal of International Law*, Vol. 94, No. 4. (Oct., 2000), pp. 773-789.

Carole Nagengast. "Violence, Terror, and the Crisis of the State." *Annual Review of Anthropology*, Vol. 23. (1994), pp. 109-136.

Jonathan Benthall. "Fox Among the Lambs." *Anthropology Today*, Vol. 5, No. 3. (Jun., 1989), 1-2.

Liisa H. Malkki. "Refugees and Exile: From "Refugee Studies" to the National Order of Things." *Annual Review of Anthropology*, Vol. 24. (1995), pp. 495-523.

Debora Shuger. "Irishmen, Aristocrats, and Other White Barbarians" *Renaissance Quarterly*, Vol. 50, No. 2. (Summer, 1997), pp. 494-525.

Kyle Grimes. "The Entropics of Discourse: Michael Harper's Debridement and the Myth of the Hero." *Black American Literature Forum*, Vol. 24, No. 3. (Autumn, 1990), pp. 417-440.

M. Estellie Smith. "The Process of Sociocultural Continuity." *Current Anthropology*, Vol. 23, No. 2. (Apr., 1982), pp. 127-142.

Controlling Racial Population Growth in a New World Order

Direct quotation from

http://en.wikipedia.org/wiki/Georgia_Guidestones (without citations)

Georgia Guidestones

From Wikipedia, the free encyclopedia
Georgia Guidestones

Chinese and Arabic inscriptions of the Georgia Guidestones

Coordinates	34.231984°N 82.894506°W
Location	Elbert County, Georgia, US
Designer	R. C. Christian (pseudonym)
Material	Granite
Height	19' 3" (5.87 m)
Opening date	March 1980

The **Georgia Guidestones** is a **granite** monument in **Elbert County**, **Georgia**, in the United States. A message clearly conveying a set of ten guidelines is inscribed on the structure in eight modern languages, and a shorter message is inscribed at the top of the structure in four ancient language scripts: **Babylonian**, **Classical Greek**, **Sanskrit**, and **Egyptian hieroglyphs**.

The structure is sometimes referred to as an "American Stonehenge".[1] The monument is 19 feet 3 inches (5.87 m) tall, made from six granite slabs weighing 237,746 pounds (107,840 kg) in all.[2] One slab stands in the center, with four arranged around it. A **capstone** lies on top of the five slabs, which are astronomically aligned. An additional stone tablet, which is set in the ground a short distance to the west of the structure, provides some notes on the history and purpose of the Guidestones.

In June 1979, an unknown person or persons under the **pseudonym** R. C. Christian hired Elberton Granite Finishing Company to build the structure.[2]

In 2008, the stones were defaced with **polyurethane** paint and graffiti with slogans such as "Death to the new world order".[3] *Wired* magazine called the defacement "the first serious act of vandalism in the Guidestones' history".[2]

A message consisting of a set of ten guidelines or principles is engraved on the Georgia Guidestones in eight different languages, one language on each face of the four large upright stones. Moving clockwise around the structure from due north, these languages are: **English**, **Spanish**, **Swahili**, **Hindi**, **Hebrew**, **Arabic**, **Chinese**, and **Russian**.

Maintain humanity under 500,000,000 in perpetual balance with nature.

The world population was estimated around 500,000,000 in **1650**

In **1650**, the 13 original American colonies weren't yet complete, and the United States of America would not become a nation until 126 years later.

1.   Virginia (1607) - Established by the London Company
New Jersey (1618) - Originally settled by the Dutch, but seized by the English in 1664.

2.   Massachusetts (1620) - Founded as two colonies:

3.   Plymouth Colony (1620), settled by the Pilgrims; and Massachusetts Bay Colony (1630), settled by the Puritans. They were united in 1691, and annexed Maine, which had been colonized by the New England Council in the 1620's.

4.   New Hampshire (1622) - Originally part of Maine, then a colony from 1629 until annexed by Massachusetts, 1641-1643. Became a separate colony again in 1679.

5.   Pennsylvania (1623) - Originally settled by Dutch and Swedes. Came under English control in the 1664 and was granted to William Penn by Charles II in 1681.

6.   New York (1624) - Founded as New Netherland by the Dutch West India Company. Seized by the English in 1664 and renamed.

7.   Maryland (1634) - Granted to Lord Baltimore.

8.   Connecticut (1635) - Founded by settlers from Massachusetts and other colonies. New Haven Colony, founded by settlers from Massachusetts in 1638, annexed to Connecticut in 1662, when the older colony was granted a royal charter.

9.   Rhode Island (1636) - Settled by two groups from Massachusetts and united in 1644. Chartered by King Charles II in 1663.

10.   Delaware (1638) - Settled by Swedes; seized by the Dutch in 1655 and by the English in 1664. Granted to William Penn in 1682.

In **1650**, American blacks were slaves, Native American Indians "owned" the land in North and South America, and the British Empire was on the rise. Is the implication that the world back then in 1650 was the ideal power relationship between empire building whites and the rest of the world inhabited by non-whites?

Population Goals for the New World Order from 2000-2100

While the 500 million Georgia Guildstones goal is likely to be unattainable without a global catastrophe like an asteroid impact or global thermal nuclear war, an environmental and eugenics approach may be on the drawing boards, if viruses fail to "trim the herd" of native peoples in resource rich continents, such as Africa, South America and Asia, comprised primarily of non-white populations.

Following is an imagined "new eugenics" plan that could be effectuated with mandatory sterilization of people in the 3rd World who have given birth to one child.

Population Limit: 2 billion humans with the goal of artificial evolution of Homo sapiens.

Once a global government is firmly in place, eugenics through genetic manipulation could create survival criteria benchmarks that will cause the artificial evolution of human beings to produce a superior species that will be enlightened, stronger, more robust for space travel, and have longer life spans free of disease. Subsequent to mandatory global population control, those who are "chosen" to live might have to reach certain standards, or they could be "recycled" into Soylent Green, a food source for commercially produced animals.

Multiphasic Survival Criteria:

All Minimum Benchmarks Must Be Achieved

Intelligence Parameters: Minimum I.Q. of 140 on Stanford-Binet Intelligence Test or

1. Combined SAT of 1100, no score lower than 500, and
2. HS G.P.A. of 3.5 on 4.0 scale or 3.6 on 5.0 scale or
3. College G.P.A. of 3.3 on 4.0 scale or
4. Top 10 percentile score on at least one skill needed by global society: art, music, spatial, math, computer, speech, dance, game design, engineering, inventing, spiritual, science, medicine and other practical aptitudes or skills.

Age Parameter: Up to 60 years old, meeting the following criteria:

1.   MRI indicates no internal disease or damage to skeletal or organs

2.   DNA test indicates no genetic defects or predisposition to disease

3.   B.P. under 125/85 on empty stomach

4.   Body fat not to exceed 20% height to weight BMI

5.   No STDs or history of dormant or incurable STD

6.   No history of drug or alcohol abuse or convictions

7.   No history of psychological or psychiatric problems

8.   No history of violence

9.   No functional disabilities (excepted as below)

All persons must meet the minimum benchmarks on an annual basis. Failure to pass benchmarks subjects individuals to a one-year probationary period requiring monthly testing and evaluation. Failure to pass benchmarks after one-year probation period subjects individual to euthanasia.

Exception to 60-year-old rule:

1. Individual possesses skills required for species advancement in science, art, technology, spirituality, philosophy, music, invention, engineering, computers, or other fundamental areas of knowledge deemed necessary for species survival.

2. Individual possesses monetary or convertible hard assets (discounting paper wealth such as stocks) exceeding 100 times the global average per capita income pegged to Y2K (estimated at $100,000 U.S.) adjusted for inflation.

3. The political, military, and economic elites may have blood relations exempted from meeting minimal requirements and will be allowed to live out natural lives; however, all such persons excepted will not be allowed to procreate.

Procreation:

1. Age Limit = 30;   Quantity Limit = 1

2. Exceptions: Global government determines areas of genetic diversity for racial quotas and fills deficiency on annual basis by issuing permits to couples or surrogate singles to have specific genotype offspring deemed necessary to species survival and advancement.

3. The goal is to keep world population at about 2 billion people, at whatever means necessary.

4. All minimal intelligence and physical ability criteria must be met by potential parents before receiving permission to have a child.

Immortality:

Eligible for cloned bodies and cerebral transplantation:

1.   Individuals who attain MENSA status (top 2% of population)

2.   Individuals who perform physical tasks at top 5% of population   3.   Individuals possessing skills per exceptions above

4.   Individuals possessing assets per exceptions above

5.   Individuals who are deemed "beautiful" (top 1% of population)

Technology that will permit pervasiveness of "Big Brother"

1980s: Robotics introduced to auto building assembly lines

1990s: Cell phone explosion, voice recognition email, and proliferation of ISPs and free email

2000:   Interactive voice recognition phone trees. PCs increased processing speed by a factor of 40 times within 10 years; chip memory quadruples [squared] to 128K. Data transmission speed increase due to hardware improvements. Dotcom crash.

2010:   First World optical fiber network in place and secured and data transmission speed increase by 1000x due to optic fiber network. Voice recognition linked to robotic equipment. Integrated cell phones with GPS wireless telecommunication proliferate. Bio-computer microchips linked to GPS, real time data storage and retrieval, with built in automatically scanned "walk-in, walk-out" purchasing software.

2012: You can run, but you can't hide. The repeal of privacy laws, and installation of the secret "Big Brother" computer.

The Projected New World Order Hierarchy

Highest Tier: USA – Germany – Britain – Canada – Australia - Japan

Second Tier: Russia – France – Western Europe – Israel

Third Tier: Asia – China, Japan, So. Korea, Taiwan, Singapore, Latin America, Mexico, Africa – Ghana, South Africa, Middle Eastern Arab Nations

Fourth Tier: Developing Nations in Asia, Latin America, Central Asia, Africa

Fifth Tier: Global Undeveloped and Impoverished Nations, such as No. Korea, Myanmar, Borneo, etc.

Developments Leading to the New World Racial Order

Political

1. U.S. Hegemony – As long as China and Japan are willing to support America's deficit spending, the U.S. will continue to pour a lion's share into military technologies to maintain its hegemonic position as the global policeman protecting elitist global economic stability and security.

2. German Hegemonic Goals – The Fourth Reich is on the rise, as German ambition and economic power has risen from the ashes.

3. Demise of Britain – The English have retrenched since WWII to their island domain, and the Rothschild's have welded their banking power all the way into Buckingham Palace.

4. China's Balancing Act – China's economic and military ambitions are supposedly directed inward, however it's been apparent that the U.S. is somewhat apprehensive. China is making dependable trading partners globally, and both European and American investments have made China into a capitalistic profit-making engine for the international elites.

5. Russian Resurgence – While Russia is unlikely to reconstitute a communist Soviet Union, its ethnic ambitions will continue to drive a wedge between its leaders and the west. Russia has numerically more nukes than the U.S., with Israel third, Britain, France, and China comprising the major nuclear powers. Don't underestimate Putin and the Russians.

6. Rise of Islamic Extremism – Muslims are rising in power even as the U.S. attempts to keep them in check. They sit on oil reserves that will make them important to the global economy even as the west disagrees with their religious dogma and mistreatment of women. As more Islamic children from war torn Arab lands come into adulthood, the west should expect the continued escalation of terrorism.

7. Domestic & Global Terrorism – There is a building undercurrent of resentment and hatred for the elites who rule the world through their surrogate governments. This hatred is spawned by the extreme dichotomy between the rich and the poor. When the poor have nothing left to lose, but everything to gain, you bet they will attack the symbols and property belonging to the wealthy elites.

8. Other Significant Global Actors – There have been no major globally respected leaders since Nelson Mandela, but every generation seems to produce a "man of the people" who is able to galvanize the faceless masses to political action against the status quo.

9. Politics of Oil Supply Manipulation – The price of oil and other energy products is not only subject to the forces of supply and demand, as producers can fluctuate the price of oil to maximize their profits by reducing their supplies below market demand.

10. Political & Bureaucratic Reform – Corruption is rampant at all levels of government in most nations in the world. As long as government is obsessed with making deals in secret, this problem will continue. Whistle blowers are labeled as traitors for exposing government secrets and wrong doings that shouldn't have been done in the first place. Government will

11. never gain the trust of the people they are entrusted to protect as long as it is not transparent and remains secretive.

12. Environmental Impact – As population continues to increase, greater developmental pressure is created that results in environmental pollution, ecological degradation, and adverse climatic changes. There are those whose perspective on population control is similar to that typified by animal shelters... euthanasia. Let's hope they don't become the global rulers in the New World Order.

Economic

1. Oil & Energy Market Manipulation – Shortages will be artificially created as an excuse to exploit untapped oil in Africa.

2. Stock Market Manipulation – Stock markets will be intentionally crashed, so the elites who have converted much of their wealth to gold can go back in to take advantage of penny stocks like Facebook

3. Corporate Corruption – Besides "cooking" their books like major movie studios, CEO's will use smoke and mirrors accounting to hide their real compensation and wealth.

4. Effects of Bureaucratic Reform – People will finally rise up against inefficient, ineffective, and insensitive bureaucracy and demand greater accountability, such as what is happening with the V.A. Adm.

5. Internet Commerce – E-commerce will outpace "brick and mortal"
6. Corporate Downsizing – As more is done via high speed Internet, less office space and employees are needed.
7. Unemployment Pandemic – Coupled with increased use of robotics and Internet solutions to almost everything, jobs will become scarce.
8. Acts of Terrorism – More mentally ill and jihadists will make their presence known, and people accept it as another part of modern life
9. Environmental Impact – Population pressures continue to erode the environment, exacerbating all consequential problems.

Social

1. Mass Media Manipulation – Information becomes controlled by a few mega media corporations with political agendas, to manipulate public opinions through fear mongering or mindless programming.
2. Educational Reforms – On-line education by top educators reaching millions reduce necessity for classroom instruction and teachers.
3. Bifurcation of Classes – Only two classes remain, the super rich and everyone else.
4. Feminist Agenda – Females push through the glass ceiling and become as ruthless, nepotistic, and exploitative as men.

5. Racial Politics – NPO's deliver racial block votes as society becomes more racially segregated by neighborhoods, counties, and states.

6. Political Agenda – Government whistle blowers release confidential emails among global economic and power elites exposing their collusion to foment warfare for corporate profits.

7. Civic Capital – People get fed up, and more join community groups to exert pressure on government corruption and laxitude.

8. Privacy & Spying – Totally out of control and not protected by Supreme Court rulings who decide the U.S. Constitution does not prohibit spying, and it's up to individual citizens to shield themselves.

9. Government Controls & Laws – Society enters a neo-fascists era, where due to Supreme Court ruling against privacy "rights", people become wary of exercising free speech and free press.

10. Cloning and Genetic Modifications – Great strides, in-fetal enhancements, and disease corrections.

Science & Technology

1. Computer Technology Advancements -

2. Genetic Engineering - Including xeno-human hybrids, artificial genetic eugenics to progressive evolve the human species. Discovery of the immortality codon through epigentics.

3. Bio-Technology Advancements – Humans become like cars, with customized spare parts manufactured to replace old or damaged ones. Solutions to balding, aging, obesity, and other concerns.

4. Energy Technology Advancements – Efficient residential and commercial building energy stations combining solar, wind, and hydrology (water in pipes and drainage turns electric motors).

5. Robotics Advancements and Applications – A.I. wed to robots create humanoids who respond more effectively than humans.

6. Spying Technology Pervasiveness – Micro dots everywhere that see and hear via cloud connectivity to spy platforms.

7. Space Exploration – Extra rocket engines put in orbit around Earth, Moon, and Mars to reduce travel time to 2 months RT, and enable planetary exploration.

8. Deep Ocean Exploration – Super submarines with titanium, carbon fiber, Kevlar composite hulls withstand the deepest pressures.

9. Planetary Deterioration – Development and poaching result in the extinction of 90% of all animal and plant species.

10. Near Space Objects – A international global system to detect NEO's becomes operational.

Religious

1. Conflict and Confluence with Scientific Knowledge – Vatican and secret government files are leaked with proof God is an alien being as stated in the Bible. He is not a spirit, but a living entity.

2. Resistance to Substantive Change – The elites pull out all the stops to maintain the status quo and their supremacy.

3. Inter-religious Conflict – True believers fight each other to the death as western nations fight zealot Islamists.

4. Extraterrestrial Contacts – The proof cannot longer be hidden.

5. Discovery of method to measure the existence of "the soul" – A new technology that creates a "plasma bubble" around a dying person is able to "capture a person's soul" and is digitally measured and recorded.

Event Horizon

1. Political – The global elites push for the elusive One World Order. Private ownership of nation-states is recognized by the U.N.

2. Economic – The "one percenters" increase their ownership stake in global wealth, land and resources to 80%.

3. Social – People minimize contact with others as technology becomes the social safety buffer as violence increase… virtual life is the norm.

4. Science & Technology – Great advances in all aspects of science as computer technology and robotics wed to "invent" new technologies and make scientific discoveries without the need for humans.

5. Religious – Educated people conclude organized religion is primarily monetary exploitation, and religious books and mythologies are actually historical records and interpretations of past events.

6. Extraterrestrials – We will finally meet our makers, but the results won't be good for humanity. It will become a war of the worlds.

Predictions

1. Globalization – The digital Internet world make real time global interactions and trade the norm, as corporations flee to off-shore tax havens to avoid paying their fair share of taxes.

2. Secret World Government – Certain members will attempt to show their faces to declare and install the New World Order.

3. Extraterrestrial Collusion – Whistle blowers leak documents that confirm extraterrestrial "Fallen Angels" had been assisting the Nazis during WWII to create WMD's because they hate Jews.

4. Self-Fulfilling Prophecy – World leaders are able to control the flow of information on the Internet to manipulate global populations.

5.   The Final Conflict – Every species eventually
becomes extinct. Human beings, as other species
and cultures, go through the natural stages of birth,
discovery, growth, plateau, decline, obsolescence,
and demise or destruction. Maybe Homo sapiens will
self-destruct by the end of this century?

The world is taking strides toward the creation of the one
world order where
certain powerful groups of the financial elites are able to own world
leaders who make new laws to further empower the elites. Third
world nations with their non-white populations will be the casualties
as private armies will supplant regional governments. Biogenetic
weapons, such as biochemical and viral attacks will be unleashed in
resource rich regions to depopulate humans so corrupt privatized
governments can hand over the land and its resources to the
corporate elites.

Implementing The New World Order Timeline

The history of the world has always been the struggle for
dominance between the powerful and the relatively powerless. A
dynamic life and death balance occurs at all levels of life, from
viruses to humans, just as it had once existed among dinosaurs and
earliest life. Are mankind's problems part of natural selection? Has
the hand of divine intervention been no more than an innate human
desire for benevolent paternalism? And if so, is the human desire to
believe in gods or a monotheistic God based on a psychological fear

of the harsh environment that has always been naturally filled with violence and danger over time? And if there is such an superior intelligent entity as God, why should that presumption exclude the existence of lesser gods, defined as intelligent living beings who are superior to humans? If God exist, why isn't it at least probable that humans have been, continue to be, and will in the future be visited by gods, not all of whom want to embrace and love humans, but rather to dominate us, as in the past?

Simple math and science relative to cosmology indicates that the earth is no more than 5.5 billion years old, orbiting a lesser star, the sun, in the outer quadrant of the Milky Way, a lesser galaxy in the outer quadrant of a visible universe that is 12-15 billion years old. Primates that may be relatives to humans appeared on earth about a mere 4.5 million years ago. The visible universe contains over 100 billion billion galaxies, each containing over 100 billion stars. We are infants in the scope of time, in the breath of life. Once again, our ethnocentrism tries to justify that we are the center of intelligent life, yet human history and contemporary affairs has repeatedly proven that we are not very intelligent, and definitely not particularly wise or humane as a species. What other species makes it a routine activity to kill its own kind in massive numbers, and to exterminate millions of other species, whether deliberately or inconsiderately?

Viewed from space, humans are like a disease, overrunning and killing everything, animals, plants, and the ecosystem. And we feel justified, a manifest destiny to spread our need to explore and dominate into space, to other planets. And what will humans likely do, should we finally figure out how to get "there"? Probably the same program as we have on Earth. Plunder, exploit, extract, destroy, and kill anything that gets in the way, just as the program against the 3rd World has been effected since Europe's boom days in exploration led to imperialism, colonialism, neo-colonialism, and now globalization. How close we are to global thermal nuclear war is a subject of debate and secret preparations by paranoid governments who attempt to protect their assets from other states and "terrorists." Perhaps the smallest life forms, the bacteria will reclaim the Earth from humans, by catastrophic plague from which no known anti-biotic is effective. That might be a good thing for the planet, though not good for Homo sapiens.

Since the development of city-states evolved into nation-states, various forms of government were created to give dominance and economic advantage to elite classes of humans. In the quest and justification of social order and peace, states have gone to war thousands of times, killing over a billion people over time. Empires, kingdoms, and dynasties still exist, but in modern form, renamed with more eloquent terms, like democracy and socialism. The elite 10% of humans still own or control 90% of the land and resources of our planet, and in too many cases, that includes ownership of human beings as slaves, serfs, and indentured servants who are exploited at low wages, for crime, or prostitution to enrich the coffers of their "employers". No matter what nation we look to, the game is the same, only the names change.

The rich exploit the poor. The poor are too busy trying to survive meager lives to organize for better rights, as they have become sheep, afraid of the wolves, the police, para-military, and military whose primary job is to protect the equity owners in their respective nations, not to protect people. Only a fool would feel more secure when as a commercial jetliner passenger, one sees the jet fighter escorts off its wing tips. The escorts' job is to shoot down the commercial jet, should there "appear" to be a threat the jet will be used instead as a bomb. Suicidal "terrorists" or deranged individuals care little if they are killed in the course of acting out their agenda against the public, and a glorified death is their primary goal.

If the role of military jets is now to shoot down commercial jets, then every passenger should be issued parachutes and briefed on their use as part of boarding and emergency information dispensed by flight attendants. But that would cost too much for airlines. Once again, a price has been placed on human life, so the common religious thought that human life is precious and priceless is a lie, otherwise its followers would practice that value. The scientists are probably more realistic in stating that a human being's trace elements are worth less than ten dollars in carbon compounds. Or maybe a convicted felon from a Chinese prison is worth the cost of his transplantable parts, which to that convict or political prisoner becomes a negative incentive, worth a couple of hundred dollars to the state.

And now, we have a czar of homeland security in America. We should know that any bureaucracy that has been created is likely to grow, to usurp more power, and to jealously guard their jurisdiction. The history of organizational behavior indicate that its actors will refuse to relinquish power and budget, once its been given. What will the evolution of homeland security become? Will citizens be required to organize "building watch", "school watch", and "job watch" as a more pervasive and ominous form of current day voluntary "neighborhood watch"? How did the "SS" begin in pre-WW2 Germany? Perhaps citizens, for "their own protection" will be required to carry "national identification cards", a "smart-card" with intrusive personal, financial, and medical information, encoded and assessable only to banks, insurance companies, and the government. And what logically comes after the "smart card"? Computer chip implants?

We need to look no further than recent history to see the effects of both state-sponsored proactive terrorism, mass-based reactive terrorism, and individually-based Kamikaze terrorism. The seeds of rebellion and terrorism have been planted by state-sponsored or supported terrorism that is the common legacy of imperialism, colonialism, neo-colonialism, and corrupt regimes. There are no "truly innocent" parties, and no "true victims" in acts of terrorism. Neither non-combatants nor military personnel can claim neutrality. To the degree that they benefit, even those who benefit, however slightly, from the economic, political, and military policies of states that oppress other peoples, is in a way complicity "not innocent" of the consequences of such policies, and is "not innocent" of the logical and predictable consequences and rebellion that invariably and inevitably result as desperate reactions to oppression and great disparities.

So how is the world going to get out of this latest round of terrorism? Will "smoking out terrorist", and "getting them on the run" truly solve the root causes of terrorism? Or will harsh military and economic policies and disparate globalization serve to galvanize a new and even deadlier generation of suicidal religious zealots. The "kill" ratio of 19 terrorist was about 6,000 in the WTC incident of 9-11-01. If that rate can be sustained by 1,900 terrorist, then 600,000 people would be killed. If 19,000 terrorists, 6,000,000 people could die (the same number of people murdered during the Holocaust). If 190,000 terrorists, 60,000,000 people could be killed. But we're only talking about flying jets into skyscrapers. Bio-terrorism or nuclear terrorism would undoubtedly up the ante and "kill ratio". Maybe that's part of the plan.

The survival of mankind will depend on fundamentally changing the elitist global system that supports and enforces the grossly inequitable distribution of economic resources to the great suffering of the poor. But will the rich voluntarily give up their power and wealth? Never. But might the elites consider paradigm changes if it could be proven that their short term, and especially long-term need for social and political stability could be better served by changing specific facets of the world system? Possibly.

Impending global paradigm changes can be seen on the event horizon that will alter the manner in which humans related to each other, and how nation-states deal with the global village, and its own domestic affairs. The possible outcomes are many, and the extreme consequences could either be human extinction, or human enlightenment, nuclear and genetic war killing billions of people, or consensual interaction and engagement leading to long lasting peace and prosperity for all. Or there may be "external" extraterrestrial forces that will create a complete realignment of human perceptions and values, whether that would be in the form of an "Armageddon" sized asteroid or returning of the "gods", no one can predict. We shall know, when we can know.

The impending paradigm changes are many, cross several disciplines, and will invariably have interactive effects on almost all aspects of life. Elitism versus powerlessness has been institutionalized and woven into cultures as classism, racism, ethnic bias, religious intolerance, and genderism that has resulted in great suffering and poverty for exploited and debased people. Governance and organizational structure and power has been hierarchical, centralized, and unequal instead of decentralized, horizontally multi-tiered, and consensual that encourages power sharing instead of concentration. The world economic system is based on pure profit, with little or no regards for resource depletion or inhumane human exploitation and disparities. The elites' vision of a completely integrated global market, controlled by a relatively small group of MNC's, owned by a handful of elites, who in collusion control every nation-state on the planet, is a twisted idea based on wanton greed and profiteering from other peoples' grief. It is unclear at what point the masses will rebel, or whether they may acquiesce to authority, as in the United States. It is unclear if the elites will someday unleash their technological and military might to kill 4 billion poor people, to "cleanse" the world of poverty, leaving a world with a dichotomy, those inhabitants who rule, and those who purpose is to serve those who rule.

Technological advances are even now pushing the envelope in science and will impact global social, political, military and economic systems in a wide range of areas within the next decade. New sources of renewable energy, genetic manipulation, "clean" weapons of mass destruction, extra-low-frequency (ELF) mind-control methods, climatic disruptions or control, and space exploration will pressure the status quo to adjust and to integrate the impending changes into their global system of profiteering. Will the result be greater control on the minds, hearts, and souls of human beings? Or will something better emerge? I hope the later, but if history is a teacher, then I fear the former. Let's hope for a quantum improvement in the quality of life, with an increase in purposefulness, and a de-emphasis on materialism and consumerism. Let's pray for peace and stability through education and empowerment, to avoid more violence.

Possible Chronology for Global Population Control and Genocide

1980s: Robotics introduced to auto building assembly lines, resulting in higher efficiency, but drastically decreasing the number of higher paid workers. Corporate executive incomes average 100 times that of average workers. Surveillance technology becoming more popular as a crime prevention tool.

1990s: Cell phone explosion revolutionizes communications potential. Voice recognition technology improving, allowing vocal email recognition. Proliferation of ISPs and free email supports a boom in the dotcom sector. The pre-Y2K hype pumps half a trillion

dollars into the technology market as the "fix", encouraging uncontrolled stock market speculation by average citizens, boosting the value of stocks duringY2K. Surveillance technology becomes more pervasive as it becomes miniaturized.

2000: Interactive voice recognition phone trees replace receptionists, phone operators, and customer service representatives for major corporations. PCs increase processing speed by a factor of 40 times within 10 years and chip memory quadruples [squared] to 128K. Digital data transmission speed and bandwidth and fiber optics greatly increase the limits communications. The dotcom crash sucks half a trillion dollars out of retirement funds, and leaves the average retiree more broke than before Y2K.

2001: As the world begins to slip into an economic recession, terrorists strike at the heart of the world's financial center, setting back the U.S. economy for several months. As the mighty American-British Armada strike at the few assets of one of the second poorest and most desolate nation-states in the world, terrorists retaliate against U.S. owned or supported targets all over the world. The nations of the North respond defensively, and follow the American program of "homeland defense". Border controls are tightened. Citizens allow greater surveillance, search, and arrest powers to the state, further limiting constitutional protections. The economic markets are on a roller coaster ride.

2002: New investment opportunities are exploited for security and military technologies. A new generation of surveillance, eavesdropping, sniffing, testing, and "early warning" systems become available to corporations, government, and individuals who can afford them. The world economy stabilizes as incidents of terrorism decreases, and appears to be under control. A few incidents of car bombs, but nothing major, and there's no lasting peace between Israel and Palestine. Russia's economy still suffers and resentment against the West increase, as billions of economic aid never reach the impoverished masses.

2003: Coordinated biological terrorist attacks via the mail are attempted by terrorists. Intelligence information suggests Sadaam Hussein as the supplier of the biological substances. The U.S. fails to gain the support of the Arab world for military action, and NATO, against the wishes of the UN, unilaterally bombs Iraq's military facilities, taking out his biological, chemical, and nuclear capacity, killing Sadaam and his top generals. A power vacuum arises in Iraq, and the U.S. repatriates half of the 8,000 Iraqis who had been living in the U.S., and sets up a puppet government in Iraq.

2004: The Iranians and Syrians feel they are next on the hit list. On the surface, they pretend to cooperate with the North, in exchange for economic aid. Surreptitiously, they support various groups who wish to destabilize the North. They make secret deals with certain rouge KGB agents and individuals in the Russian Mafiya to purchase nuclear weapons. Our intelligence network discovers the plot. A secret plan is made to retrieve the nukes.

When Special Forces fail to recover all the nukes, and several teams are captured or killed the U.S./NATO pact strike Iran and Syria, then install puppet governments. To prevent future terrorism, all citizens are mandated to carry a national identification "smart card".

2005:   Great strides are made in stem cell research and the first human being is successfully cloned (after several dozen failed and deformed fetuses are disposed). A complete head transplant is made, and stem cells permit the reattachment of the spinal nerves. Stem cell technology permit paralyzed people to regain the ability to function without machine assistance. Cold fusion and essentially frictionless gravity propelled technologies prove to be feasible, causing a new   boom in energy investments. Big oil interests attempt to block the new technology, but it is bigger than big oil, who then attempt to retool and reinvest in new wave energies. The West controls the oil production in Iraq, Iran, and Syria. The Saudi's and other oil producers capitulate to Western price controls, and see their wealth decrease as China's exploitation of reserves in the China Sea cut their demand.

2007:   First World optical fiber network in place and secured, and data transmission speed   increases by 1000x due to optic fiber network. Voice recognition linked to robotic equipment that has been miniaturized as intelligent multi-functional "slaves." Millions   of workers' have their jobs replaced by computer and robotics technologies. Citizens in MDC's are hard pressed to find jobs, and they fall into hard times. The world falls   into a deep economic recession and regional depression, with worldwide rebellion.

2018:   Civil unrest in the West increase, commensurate with mass insurrection in Third World puppet states, as unemployed, suffering, and impoverished masses seek to attack the symbols of the elites. The West mandates all employed citizens to take the computer "low-jack" implant as a strategy to control insurrection. The elites release a secret genetically engineered food-borne virus into genetically modified foods. Those who agreed to receive the "low-jack" chip are able to obtain untreated food from special government regulated stores or delivery services. The food virus has an incubation period of 6 months, and 4 billion people become inauspiciously infected. Symptoms include loss of appetite, vomiting, and general malaise. Death occurs due to starvation. It's non-infective to non-consumers, but infected foods are given as humanitarian aid by the U.N.

2019:   Western governments pretend to be feverishly working on a cure for the food virus, now dubbed "poor man's disease". The secret vaccine is locked in government safes. 2 billion people die after the 6 months incubation period. No cure is in sight.

2020: Northern governments feel a cure for "poor man's disease" is close at hand. Another 2 billion people die during the first six months of the year, after which the miracle "cure" is released to the public. The genetically engineered food virus is removed from the food chain. The world's population stands at 2.5 billion people, of which 1 billion reside relative disease free in the North (comprised 95% of whites), 500 million in White Russia, Middle East, and Central Asia, 500 million in China, Japan, India, and advanced Asian nations. The remainder 500 million people inhabit Latin America, of which less than 50 million are still alive in Africa. The North divides the territories in Africa into reconstruction zones, to exploit its virgin territories for expansive mineral deposits.

2021: As the world begins to recover its economic balance, with a reduced, but more efficient economic distribution system, most industrial assets remain in place. Among the elites, few were affected by "poor man's disease", and they continue to rule their nation-states. They negotiate and cooperate among each other for the planned utilization of planetary resources, both human, non-human, and inanimate. The elitist paradigm of a global economy with exclusive control of resource exploitation and distribution is near at hand.

2026: An international team, comprised of an American, Brit, Russian, and Chinese orbit Mars. Evidence of possible subterranean intelligent civilizations is suppressed. MDC's convert to new energies, while LDC's are sold the oil from the Middle-East. Big Oil earns even more profits, with one foot in each energy technology, old and new. Another quantum leap in computer miniaturization, processing speed, and memory permits the development of wristwatch sized voice activated computers with global wireless connection. People can walk, see, talk, and understand anyone with a similar device anywhere in the world. The world continues to become more dichotomously accentuated between the rich and the poor, both internally and externally to the North versus the Third World. News begins to leak in the scientific community about Martian life.

2032: In the course of exploiting deep into Africa's subsoils in search of minerals needed for high tech computers, robotics, and space exploration, an unknown bacteria is released   that is highly transmittable and persistent through air, liquids, and solids. The bacteria's rapid spread is sudden and unabated. National labs took an entire week to diagnose it as a new biological agent, but by that time, 2 billion people die, including half of the one million ruling elite. The rest of humanity's existence hangs in the balance. Mankind is only a week from extinction. Several hundred babies are born at the last moments as humans take their last dying breaths. From the heavens, UFO's appear. They take the last vestiges of the human species into their space crafts and fly off into outer space.

2033: The plants and animals on planet Earth begin to replenish the world. Natural forces again respond to a dynamic balance once lost to humans. Once populated human cities, state symbols, great air forces, and naval armadas become wreckage and is recycled as shelter for animals, birds, and sea creatures. Vegetation eventually overgrows even the highest skyscrapers. From space, the planet appears serene, as a revolving jewel, once again as it had previously been for billions of years.

2014: Then again, there could be other scenarios that resolve world problems by dealing fairly   with the root causes of violence, which are disempowerment, poverty, intolerance, and fanaticism. Each is a cause of the other, as powerlessness is usually expresses as impoverishment, which in turn abets intolerance and a rise of fanaticism, whether based on religious or political ideology. The root of all evils in human history can be traced directly or indirectly to the wanton greed and hoarding of power by the elites of the world. Until the elites are willing to relent in their avarice, the masses in the world will feel justified in attacking elitist symbols and nation-states by any means necessary.

Chapter 3 – Institutionalized race

Racial inequities will become institutionalized in the new world economic and political order for several reasons, including:

- The entrenched power and economic elites will resist changing the global financial and global trade paradigm that has guaranteed them wealth.
- Existing national economic inequities that already exist will persist.
- National and regional economies are pieces of puzzles on the global board game of economic dominance and power brokering that maintains benefits and the advantageous financial structure for the wealthy elites.
- The general distribution of races into specific economic roles in specific niches in the global economic machine reflects existing global racial paradigm, of which the American racial landscape is a representational microcosm. For example, the poorest people are Africans, and in by comparison to whites and other races in America, blacks account for a disproportionately high representation of the poor. Asians are second only to whites in terms of financial success, both globally and in the U.S. The Hispanics are generally the lower middle class or poor both globally and in America, but on the whole do better than African-Americans and Africans. Other ethnic groups such as Jews and Arabs and other Middle East ethnic people are not considered a race per se.

The Advance of Globalization

Many people are beginning to understand that the ultimate goal of globalization is not only economic and cultural, but political and racial. In order to understand the current and future effects of globalization, we must ask several basic questions, including:

Perplexing questions abound about globalization:
1. Where does the world stand now?
2. Who and what groups are behind it?
3. Who stands to gain and who will lose?
4. Structural changes and pre-conditions.
5. Is globalization good for humanity?
6. Despots, democracy, or destruction?
7. How could globalization benefit everyone?

What groups are accelerated developments in the globalization game? What are the pre-conditions, pros and cons, and probable scenarios, consequences, and outcomes that need to be explored? Which groups stand to benefit the most economically and politically from globalization? What structural changes will signal the onset of the One World Order through the configuration of globalization that is not too far off in our developing future? What are the facts, trends, players and consequences of this globalization game?

1. Evaluation of current degree and breadth of globalization.
2. MNC's, elites, trade brokers, governments, secret international organizations), NGO's.

3. The elites versus the poor.
4. Economic, political, cultural, religious, and environmental impact of globalization.
5. Efficient and effective global distribution versus hoarding and exploitation.
6. New World Order, the UN, diplomacy, world vision, and the ultimate military options.
7. An ideal world, happiness, peace, and global cooperation is a potential reality.

The Impending New World Order

In the period since the U.S.A. entered WW2 in 1941, the world has witnessed human atrocities against humans on a level never before recorded in history, including dropping two nuclear bombs, concentration camps, and genocide. The violence that followed WW2 was in many ways equally abhorrent, if not more so. The civil rights struggles, the Vietnam War, assassinations of JFK, MLK, RFK, MalcomX, Gandhi, and many lesser known patriots and humanitarians set the stage for contemporary state and non-state acts of violence.

The horrific inhumanity of the Jewish Holocaust was only a few decades later followed by Pol Pot's Khmer Rouge slaughter of perhaps 8 million Cambodians. Idi Amin was known to laugh out loud when slaughtering hundreds of thousands of his own people in Uganda, the Tutus and Hutus killed each other in Rwanda, and China has witnessed the executions, imprisonment, and torture of millions. It has not been a peaceful world, as technology has both advanced the efficiency and effectiveness of violence, despite the so called Cold War nuclear deterrence.

Atrocities fostered or sponsored by Western political/military elites continued, who while espousing grand humanitarian ideals, have often betrayed the very principles they pretend to profess. Isn't the life of an African, or Asian, or Jew equally worth that of a Briton, American, German, or Swede? I surmise from standard of living statistics, that in the scales of the First World Hegemon, the answer is an emphatic "NO." Therein lies the basis of the international struggle between peoples, races, and ethnic groups. American history provides prime examples of First World tactics, as the genocide of Native Americans followed a pattern of false promises, broken treaties, and military violence, and African-Americans still suffer poverty, violence, and disease in alarmingly disproportionate levels, almost 140 years after slavery was abolished in the United States of America.

What does the First World Hegemon want that entails tolerance of inhumanity in non-white states, often supporting oppressive regimes in Third World nations, which it attempts to prevent in Europe? The historical colonialist mentality still runs strongly through the blood lines of Europe's elites; only the revisionist strategy for world domination no longer lies in direct military confrontation, but in global economic control and domination, juxtaposed by military intimidation. Their vision continues to be one of a united Europe as the center of civilization, a feat first attempted by European royalty, and now made possible by the creation of multi-national corporate conglomerates owned by European and American elites. What they weren't able to accomplish with real people, they now are achieving through fictional entities (legal immortal corporations) and the utilization of technology.

Europe is in fact no more than a fictional continent created to satisfy an egomaniacal self-aggrandizing overcompensating need to deny their early backward and warring heritage. Europe is not physically a continent, but merely the western end of the Asian continent. This drive to create fictional entities (corporations), fictional (and worthless) global debtor monetary systems, deceptive and untruthful marketing, political, and bureaucratic institutions and ideals are all part of their larger scheme of world domination. The First World Anglo-Germanic European-American plan for world domination is essentially the same in principle as it was when "The sun never set on the British Empire", only the methods have been disguised and repackaged to appear beneficial to the peace and economic progress of the developing world. It's a sales pitch that is leading the Third World eventually to genocide.

The smoke screen for the new world order is the accelerating dependency of developing world markets on the Western monetary system, the creation of a future justification for military intervention to protect Western assets, and the future wholesale rape of third world resources as repayment to World

Bank members. The gradual genocide of Third World peoples through poverty, disease, racism, class warfare, violence, and military interventions (conventional, genetic, and nuclear) are methods of genocide. At the rate AIDS is decimating the population in Sub-Saharan Africa, NATO and UN troops, backed by First World corporate interests, will be called on in the future to "stabilize" Africa's infrastructure, as a pretext to develop its vast stores of natural resources for western products and consumption. The "silk road" to the eventual rape of Africa will be carved by bulldozers and the tracks of military vehicles. Most scholars whose work, when interlinked, supports the primary hypothesis that the First World's intentions and actions result in the genocide of Third World people.

Few politicians or academicians will publicly admit or profess to discern the reality that stares down humanity today, and the likely outcomes of global political-economic policies dictated by the First World bloc of nations that comprises the white race. Their methods of self-propagation are many, including technological advantage, genetic weapons, economic destabilization, cultural imperialism, and first strike nuclear projection. Is it their goal to eventually limit world population to 2 billion humans, comprised of 1 billion whites (Alphas), and 1 billion colored races (Betas)? Is their hidden agenda to rid the world of the poor, illiterate, disabled, retarded, and non-elites over 50 that comprises over 80 percent of the planet's colored races?

Applying a global market economy paradigm, the Betas would serve the Alphas by producing goods and services from industries owned by the Alphas. According to Marxist theory, the Alphas would own the means of production, and the Betas would supply the labor. The Alphas (boursequoise) would obtain the best, with the lesser grade products available to the Betas (workers class). This "ideal" configuration will save the planetary environment by eliminating pollution from developing nations, massive waste products of human consumption, and the depletion of natural resources by an exploding world population (projected to reach 30-50 billion by 2100, if supportable by earth). The world would become relatively stable because the white hegemony of so-called democratic states will be able to manage world resources according to the WTO & World Bank "standards." Developing nations, weakened by AIDS and diseases from GM (genetically modified) foods, will depend on the West to assist them, which will instead present a Trojan horse, the appearance of benign humanitarian aid, laced with genetic disease, political corruption, and economic dependency.

I.   The First World Hegemon's Anti-Third-World Genocide Strategy

        A.   Economic dominance by the World Bank; dependency of developing nations' economies under the threat of monetary destabilization. The west is waiting for AIDS to decimate and weaken African and Asian governments to the point they may step in to "restore order and for humanitarian reasons", install corrupt puppet governments, and then export the natural resources of those continents while enslaving their peoples to supply cheap labor for products of western consumption.

B. Cultural imperialism via the Internet, music, movies, clothing, food, and other deceptive marketing ploys to "sanitize" the world of non-western ideas, customs, cultures, and religions that do not conform to the ideal profit making motive of the globalized market system.

C. Political colonialism via infectious spread of "scientific management" and other western legal and bureaucratic concepts, and through bribery and corruption of developing world governmental elites. Utilization of food and medicines as coercive strategies.

D. Military domination by embargo of developing nuclear states, supporting destabilization of non-cooperative states, projecting secret genetic and viral warfare materials into the Third World (e.g., AIDS, genetically modified foods), developing a nuclear missile shield, and targeting nukes at developing Third World nations as future nuclear extortion.

The projection of First World nuclear and economic power against the Third World are parts of a secretly formulated strategy to give world dominance and control to Euro-America. History and contemporary events indicate that there exist a real (secret), though subtle conspiracy among the Anglo-Germanic elites (and their white American descendants) who control world resources to maintain their superior position through policies that directly or indirectly result in the genocide of the world's non-whites.

References:

1. Christopher Keith Hall. "The First Five Sessions of the UN Preparatory Commission for the International Criminal Court (in Current Developments)." *American Journal of International Law*, Vol. 94, No. 4. (Oct., 2000), pp. 773-789.
2. Carole Nagengast. "Violence, Terror, and the Crisis of the State." *Annual Review of Anthropology*, Vol. 23. (1994), pp. 109-136.
3. Jonathan Benthall. "Fox Among the Lambs." *Anthropology Today*, Vol. 5, No. 3. (Jun., 1989), pp. 1-2.
4. Liisa H. Malkki. "Refugees and Exile: From "Refugee Studies" to the National Order of Things." *Annual Review of Anthropology*, Vol. 24. (1995), pp. 495-523.
5. Debora Shuger. "Irishmen, Aristocrats, and Other White Barbarians" *Renaissance Quarterly*, Vol. 50, No. 2. (Summer, 1997), pp. 494-525.
6. Kyle Grimes. "The Entropics of Discourse: Michael Harper's Debridement and the Myth of the Hero." *Black American Literature Forum*, Vol. 24, No. 3. (Autumn, 1990), pp. 417-440.
7. M. Estellie Smith. "The Process of Sociocultural Continuity." *Current Anthropology*, Vol. 23, No. 2. (Apr., 1982), pp. 127-142.

Enacting Global Racial Violence

Waltz's arguable notions compared structure in the highly centralized hierarchic domestic state versus the decentralized anarchic international environmental context of the realism paradigm. In the case of international relations, Waltz opined that state interactions, human relations, and functional differences within and between states has no real consequences, that the only factors of importance is the structural positioning of states as units that compete for survival through self-help self-propagation activities in competition with other states to determine who has the greatest degree of power (military-economic). It is the structure or positioning of power that stimulates the games states feel compelled to play to protect themselves against current and potential enemies, which determines consequences in the anarchic global disorder.

The issue of social contract per Thomas Hobbes, and how the state uses police force to intimidate its citizens to comply with its laws was discussed. Other intellectuals have written about social contract, such as Rousseau, who viewed *Social Contract* as a way to alleviate, among other things, the main cause of our evils. Rousseau felt that morals seem to be of two types: that which is moral in being "established" by "a sort of convention" as men begin to associate together, and a "political" form that is moral in the sense of being "authorized" by the consent of man as a social contract. Rousseau felt that humans exist purely as physical beings, possessed solely of physical instincts, passions, and faculties; and man originally lacked moral needs or passions, or conscious regards for their fellow humans. Waltz views states as purely physical structures, possessed solely of the instinct of self-preservation corresponding to their power position in an anarchistic world, without regards to moral needs, passions, or conscious regards for humanity.

Few politicians or academicians publicly admit the reality that oppresses humanity today, the outcomes of global political-economic policies dictated by the First World bloc of nations that comprises the white race. Their methods of self-propagation are many: technology, control of capital, cultural imperialism, neo-colonialism, genetic/biological/viral/chemical weapons, and first strike nuclear projection. Is it their goal to eventually limit world population, primarily by reducing the number of Third World people who comprise 80 percent of the human race, and account for over 95% of the world's population growth.

The justification for "trimming back" world population is two fold: 1) conserving the   planetary environment by reducing pollution from developing nations, and 2) reducing the depletion of natural resources by an exploding world population (projected to reach 30-50 billion by 2100, if supportable by earth). The world would become relatively stable because the white hegemony of so-called democratic states will be able to manage world resources according to the IMF and World Bank "standards." Developing nations, weakened by AIDS and diseases from GM (genetically modified) foods, will depend on the West to assist them, which will instead present a Trojan horse, the appearance of benign humanitarian aid, laced with genetic disease, political corruption, and economic dependency; essentially the same strategy deployed against Native Americans by the U.S. Army through the spread of smallpox in blankets.

The First World Hegemon has historically implemented an anti-Third-World genocidal strategy that continues today through economic disequilibriums and other forms of socio-economic and political-cultural displacements.   Population-to-resources, population-to-capital, racial, and cultural factors fail to explain the historical as well as the cross-national variation in economic development. Economic dominance by the IMF and World Bank reinforces dependency of developing nations' economies under the threat of monetary destabilization caused by runaway debt. As AIDS decimates and weaken Africa, and increasing becomes a major public health concern in Asia and Latin America, government debt has reached the point where many Third World nation-states are essentially owned by creditor nations through the international monetary exchange system enforced by the IMF and World Bank. The First World installs corrupt puppet governments in the Third World, and rapes the natural resources of those continents while essentially enslaving their peoples to supply cheap labor for products of western consumption.

Abernethy noted in the first quarter of 1989, elite nationals of the Third World's 15 largest debtor nations were holding US $340 billion in foreign banks, up from less than $100 billion in 1980. The elites of Third World nations who support First World economic programs are allowed to pillage and plunder their own lands, as long as their actions serves the North. In Nigeria, a stark illustration of World-Bank-designed, managed, and administered structural adjustment planning caused the currency (Naira) to devalue to $0.08 from a high of $1.80, and the creation of incentives for agrarian capital investment caused the monthly minimum wage to decline from $201 (1981) to $16 (1990). Consequently, the reliability of statistical evidence turned out by the World Bank to justify structural adjustment plans and sectored reform proposals is doubted, making the usefulness of such plans for African counties suspect. By 1988, 20 African governments accepted IMF stabilization programs and 22 had adopted World Bank adjustment policies. Austerity, currency devaluation, price reform, market discipline, and privatization ensued, resulting a massive transfer of governing power from formerly sovereign states to IMF/World Bank bureaucracies. The reality of decades of IMF/World Bank coercive economic management policies has been to drive down African living standards, and to disrupted their political, tribal, social, economic, cultural, and spiritual infrastructure.

Lubeck provides another clear example of this misbegotten IMF/World Bank strategy. In Nigeria, industries expanded rapidly during the 1970s, but later withered from lack of foreign exchange, as income once engorged by oil revenues that peaked at $25.3 billion in 1980, rapidly fell to $6.3 billion in 1986 under IMF/World Bank mandated structural adjustments. The UN's Economic Commission for Africa (ECA) insisted that the World Bank's deflationary policies destroyed Africa's productive basis for recovery, encouraged nonproductive speculation, undermined Africa's industrialization, and threatened the social fabric of African societies. The ECA strongly argued that Africa's problems were structural, arising from colonial-origin commodity system- problems that can not be resolved by short-term shock treatments.

To further exacerbate the economic problems of the Third World, western nations try to find substitutes for what it buys by advancing scientific and technological discoveries. Many less developed countries export a single crop or commodity to raise capital, in a time when capital is flowing from the poor to the rich countries ($93 billion for the years 1983-87 - World Bank), investment funds to less developed nations are very limited. Western scientific advancement stands to make Third World commodities superfluous to the North. On the other hand, First World nations dictate the retail price of oil, an essential to Third World economies. While the Institut Francais due Petrole predicts a 25 to 50 percent reduction in the cost of extracting oil, they estimate the price of crude oil will increase 65 percent. At the retail level, oil prices can rise while extraction costs fall because retail prices determined by supply (which can be manipulated) and demand (which rarely decreases). The Third World is held in a noose, which tightens as the western demand for natural resources and commodities from the South decrease due to scientific and technological advancements in the North, coupled with First World manipulated higher retail crude oil prices, that exacerbates the South's financial crisis.

Countries with high per capita incomes have comparably higher capital levels of production than those with low incomes. The countries of the Third World use relatively little capital, and those of the First World are capital rich, with most of the world's capital deposited into North America, western Europe and Japan. As the gap in per capita incomes between the rich and poor nations has increased over time, poor countries continue to fall further behind their potential. The Chinese Delegation to the U.N. argued that the condition of a nation is affected by its social system and the political and economic conditions existing domestically and internationally. They insist that it is mainly due to aggression, plunder and exploitation by the imperialists, particularly the superpowers that the Third World remains poor, adding that the widening gap between MDCs and LDCs is due to the old international economic order which increases inequalities, pursues external domination, foreign occupation, colonialism, racial discrimination, apartheid and neo-colonialism in all its forms, resulting in great obstacles to the full emancipation and progress of the developing countries.

LaRouche warns, as long as the IMF system, and its related strategies exist in their present form, regional states must avoid the ruinous effects which would result from such measures fostered by an already doomed IMF system. The needed reorganization of the international financial and monetary systems requires a structural reform in composition of categories of employment, investment, and credit-flows, to return to goals and standards which are consistent with the operating objectives of dependent governments.

The First World is based upon a *historical culture of violence*, and spreads its culture in modern times through neo-colonialism and cultural imperialism via modernization and reform programs forced or exported to the Third World as marketing ploys to "sanitize" the world of non-western ideas, customs, cultures, and religions that do not conform to the political ideology and capitalistic profit motive that drives the westernized global market system.

There exist ample historical evidence to confirm the First World is based on a culture of   violence. Early Caucasian barbarians were a cruel and violent people, preoccupied with war, and were the racial founding stock for most of northern Europe. Roman historians wrote of the pervasive violence of northern European society, noting that the Germans spent all their lives in hunting and warlike pursuits because they had "no taste for peace" but consider "war and plunder" the only honorable pursuits. Among Europeans, strength determines status, and the warrior societies were ruthless and aristocratic; in Gaul only the Druids and warriors "are of any account or consideration", as the common people were typically treated almost as slaves. The Anglo-Irish were constantly occupied by endless petty warfare, even into present day times. Their culture was typified by strong kinship loyalties, lawlessness, and predatory violence that came to characterize the English aristocracy, who "consider that nothing brings you more honor than wholesale slaughter."

The upper classes felt "superior" to the lower, and members of the wealthy bourgeoisie assumed many of the attitudes of the aristocracy, including the self-adulating notion of genetic superiority. Blatant examples of cultural imperialism based upon the notion of white racial and cultural supremacy continues to be a subliminal driving force in First World domestic and international policies. During the 1920's the racial and ethnic diversity of the American population produced a mass interest in a racial eugenics movement. Increased concern over the low fertility of the white upper classes along with paranoia over the "race suicide" of superior Anglo-Saxons led to advocacy of "positive" eugenics (including increasing the fertility of the genetically superior) and "negative" eugenics (causing the "inferior stocks" to reduce their fertility). Hodgson observes that populations are still being shaped to conform to racial or ethnic preferences and genocide, a dramatic example of such shaping, is regularly attempted.

The repression of the real or imagined violence of dissidents is also justified, and enters through violent representations in popular culture, the media, television, films, the theater, and music. The forces of development and modernization combine to destroy traditional rural life in Third World countries, resulting in a constant pressure to emigrate from rural areas. Kasarda concludes that technology has fundamental influence on a society's social organization, and although societies create innovation and technology, it is the application of technology that is the cause of social change. These subordinated groups are the historical victims of western colonialism, or a result of the way colonial empires were carved up, and the resulting conflicts between nations, peoples, and minorities, often resulted in violent suppression, even genocide. Since 1945, state-sponsored violence toward ethnic and political groups caused more deaths, injuries, and human suffering than "all other forms of deadly conflict, including international wars and colonial and civil wars". Other costs are incalculable, including the extinction of languages, cultures, and ways of life, destruction of cultural and historical treasures, and loss or damage to residences, industry, and commerce. Nagengast questioned the kind of future that newly emerging elites desire in a world order, in which the possibilities for rejecting the power of the west is unlikely, where socialism has been discredited, and where there aren't other alternatives on the horizon. How, under this predicament, will new relationships of power and knowledge emerge and be resolved?

The Chinese stated before a UN committee, "In our opinion, the primary way of solving the... problem lies in combating the aggression and plunder of the imperialists, colonialists and neo-colonialists, breaking down the unequal international economic relations, winning and safeguarding national independence, and developing the national economy and culture independently and self-reliantly in the light of each country's specific conditions and differing circumstances, and raising the living standards of the people. It is highly doubtful that the North will agree with this Chinese perception.

Political colonialism through the spread of western legal and bureaucratic concepts, and through bribery and corruption of developing world governmental elites serves to bolster First World hegemonic power through Third World surrogates, puppets, and racketeers.

The IMF/World Bank. Lubeck stated that IMF structural adjustment plans (SAPs) are externally planned, organized, and monitored, and they bypass, minimize, and privatize the former powers of the state. The crisis of the post-colonial state in Africa threatens to undermine the existing system of weakened states. The political changes are greatest in Nigeria, where between a quarter and a fifth of Africa's population lives. The alliance between the World Bank and reform-minded politicians is filled with corruption, mismanagement, waste, unrealistic crops, environmental degradation, and social tension. A new class of wealthy commercial farming strata with credit and political and commercial links to urban centers is becoming more powerful and prevalent, as peasants remain poor and powerless.

The Chinese perception of history is shared by a majority of Third World nations, and substantial numbers of Western historians, when they stated, "Social-imperialism asserts that 'only economic development with my aid can solve your population problem.' This is a ruse. It goes without saying that economic development is necessary for a country to emerge from poverty and solve its population problems. The point is that what social-imperialism calls 'economic development' is nothing but a fraud if it is not coupled with the fight against imperialism and hegemonism and a change in the unequal international economic relations.'"

Nagengast reports the crisis of present day states results from its disparate concentration of power and the contradiction between it, and the demands of disempowered peoples who have created new positions that challenge the definitions of who and what ought to be repressed. The intelligentsias of the nineteen century and leaders of nationalist movements in Europe and North America had economic reasons for what they saw as a rational, democratic movements toward modernity and capitalism. The concepts of nation and nationalism in Europe and North America are the offspring of colonial expansion, religious wars, rationalism, and capitalism that serve as justification and political legitimization for certain notions of territorial, political, and cultural unity enforced by the hegemony of liberal thought and organization. Consequently, the Nagenstate observes that "the world is in transition from strict acceptance of sovereign jurisdiction and non-intervention to more and more readiness to undertake... action, up to and including military action, that would in the past have been considered intervention in domestic affairs." Kasarda observed, "While it is true that social (e.g. religious/ethnic) and economic elites wield great power, their abilities to gain hegemony over a nation's future depend on capturing and holding the political machinery. Second, these theorists post that coalitions organized around shared self-interest combine either to exert pressure on the state or to dominate it, and the express purpose of these activities is to generate laws that divert social surplus to special interests. Olson suggests that since natural resource endowments, differences in capital stocks, cultural variation in responses to economic incentives, the features of the international system are not sufficient to explain economic development. Consequently, it would seem the institutions and policies of countries would have to be important, as the politics of the First World pervasively intrudes into the governance of the Third World.

The First World uses calculated *military intimidation*, and support destabilizing non-cooperative states in the Third World and utilizes measured force to maintain economic and political hegemony. In addition to cultural propensities for violence, the First World developed philosophical justification for the need and desirability for violence and military actions. Malkki observed that wars have created tens of millions of displaced individuals and families originating in the Third World. The causes of their plight are conflicts kept alive mostly by superpower politics and by weapons manufactured in the rich countries, who export death and destruction to the Third World in exchange for importing the natural and partly processed products of the poor countries.

According Pasqualucci, a sustaining justification of western thought is that depopulation through war appears to be a natural phenomenon, as if nature itself wishes to prevent the human pretension to eliminate war forever. Thomas Hobbes felt it perfectly legitimate to establish colonies to solve the problems raised by overpopulation, adding, "in any case, a war of conquest appears here to be perfectly legitimate... when the excess of population in his own country becomes unbearable, the Sovereign 'has to', has the duty to, 'transplant,' if he can, the excess of population in another country, whether inhabited or not, and without being obliged to ask permission from anybody.

The North fear the warnings of the prophetic philosophers, intellectuals, and speculators of their time, such as Thomas Maltus and Thomas Hobbes, who would likely support paranoid doomsday scenarios, as justification for Northern warmongering. Hobbes believed Malhusian vision, when he stated that, "The development of mankind will come to an end "when all the world is overcharged with inhabitants"... therefore the only remedy for such a state of things is once again... a war of extermination... there will be no prisoners... because the scope of such a war is precisely that of making the space of the world as void as possible of inhabitants, to the point that the most frightful war of extermination will take place one day as the "last remedy of all." In his opinion, there is no doubt that the progress of mankind will end in a universal, apocalyptic conflagration, adding, "Behind the growth of the multitude in the Third World, there seems to be a messianic impulse, a thrust, to conquer the rest of the world in order to 'regenerate' it in the name of an ideology and a religion....in that 'perpetual and restless desire of power after power, that ceaseth only in death,....'" It's only too obvious that western political thinkers believe that the most efficacious way to save the world for the North, is to make space, by eliminating the burgeoning populations of the South.

The prevailing First World view is that *overpopulation and ecological* pressures provide justification to consider and pursue surrepticious genocidal programs in the Third World. Malthus proposed a theory of overpopulation in a zero-sum game of survival, where unchecked overpopulation will eventually exhaust the world food supply. Based on Maltusian ideas, the First World has formulated the "overpopulation paradigm" that blames rapid population growth on poverty, illiteracy, and cultural propensities, typical of the Third World.

The Overpopulation Paradigm:

The UN's 1993 estimated population projected in 2020 is between 7.6 to 8.5 billion.   Cohen observed that around 10,000 year ago, there were roughly 6 million people on Earth. Today, there are more than 6 billion people. The human population increased by a factor of about 1,000 in 10,000 years.   Cohen made a similar projection applying the estimated 1995 population growth rate of 1.6 percent per year. If growth of 1.6 percent per year persists for 436 years, the population will have increased to at least 1,000 fold. If people and the planet can not absorb a tenfold, rather than a 1,000 fold increase in population size to 60 billion, then the present global growth rate cannot continue even another 150 years.   The world's population has doubled over the post-war period, from 2.5 billion in 1950 to more than 5 billion in 1990, and is likely to more than triple between 1950 and the projected total of nearly 8 billion in 2020. Tapinos reported according to the UN, in 1970, the geographic distribution of human population in the world was 30 percent in developed areas, and 70 percent in less developed areas. In 1980, the ratio changed to 24 and 76 percent. In 1990, the population distribution exceeded 80 percent in less developed nations.

The First World refuses to recognize that the solution to overpopulation is to uplift the conditions of the Third World, who they blame for causing the degradation of the planet's resources, though in fact, it is the First World that consumes over 80% of the world's resources and contributes a similar percentage to its pollution, global warming, and species extinctions.

The United States uses over half of all the raw materials consumed each year; as less than 1/15 (1970) of the world's population required more than the remaining part to maintain its overconsumptive position. As present trends continued, in 20 years, we will get much less than $1/15^{th}$ of the population, and yet we may use some 80% of the resources consumed. In 2000, the U.S. population was estimated to exceed 275 million people, compared to the world's 6.1 billion inhabitants, which accounts to approximately 4.5% of the world's population utilizing most of its nonrenewable resources.

Kremer notes demographic evidence clearly indicate that if population grows at finite speed when income is above a steady state, per capita income will rise over time. If population growth declines at high levels of income, per capita income will rise over time. However, data also suggest that higher levels of income and technology may reduce fertility by increasing wages and thus the value of time, by increasing education and the relative value of women's time. He concluded that population growth increases at low levels of income, then decreases in high levels of income.

Reacting to capitalist background and the Malthusian basis of Anglo-Saxon thinking, which viewed overpopulation as the cause of poverty, almost all developing countries favored the Marxist idea that the real cause of poverty was unequal distribution of wealth, both among and between countries, and that overpopulation was a symptom rather than a cause of the basic problem. The Third World argues that economic and social development, especially more equitable distribution of economic gains among the poorest areas, would be at least, if not more effective in reducing fertility as family-planning programs. Keyfitz explained that the less developed countries contain four-fifths of the world population, are responsible for nine-tenths of present population growth, and can expect 100 percent of the world's population growth during the first century of the new millennium. Consequently, they do not have the space, land, or the capital to support their exploding citizenry. The demand for their raw materials constituted the economic foundation on which they attempted their upward course, but scientific advances in developed nations has invented substitutes that undercut the need for Third World resources.

Wilmoth noted that the "orthodox" view of the disadvantages of rapid population growth and of the possibility for positive strategies to lower birthrates in less developed countries (LCDs) dominated political discussions of the topic during the 1960s and 1970s. The dominant theme of the articles of this era was that population growth is rapid and threatens the welfare of human beings and other species. It was thought that rapid population growth threatened the very survival of the human species, due to finite limits on the availability of resources as land, water, and fossil fuels. They concluded that population growth must somehow be brought under control, either through limitations on reproduction or through an increase in the death rate. Since growth is limited by finite resources, the only sensible solution is to limit population size to a sustainable level. The North feared that inaction will eventually lead to ecological disasters that will result in widespread famine, disease, misery, and, potentially, the extinction of the human species. Yates predicted that overpopulation and underproduction in major nations of the Third World will result in great famines and pose future questions of life and death significance to the world community.

Wilmoth believes that growth produces population pressure that accentuates the threat to the stability of world political systems. Population pressure may lead nations to press outward from their borders in search of living space, or it may foster internal political instability, leading in some cases to revolutions. Population pressure has been the cause of past wars and will continue to be a source of future conflict if population growth is not controlled, adding, "Rapid population growth is disadvantageous, as overcrowding has negative effects on the quality of human existence... producing a general deterioration in the quality of the natural and social environments of human societies. Overcrowding brings in its train a host of adverse side effects, including urban congestion, pollution, shortages of housing and recreational space, and various forms of 'social pathology' that increases the role of governments at the expense of individual liberties."

This fear of potential extinction, drives the North to the argument based on a perception that one population (or sub-population) is losing or will lose control over some vital aspect of social and political life due to its relative decrease in numbers in comparison to other groups, and consequently, a race suicide framework materializes when population growth is viewed as unfavorably to the population fearful of losing control. Without a globally coordinated concentrated effort to stabilize population size at a level far lower than currently projected, the earth's ecosystems and the living standards of increasing numbers of the world's people will deteriorate. An immediate decrease in world population growth will provide time to make necessary changes, and to develop new technologies and alternative energy sources.

Brundtland reports that ninety percent of the world's population increase is occurring in developing countries, many of which are unable to feed their present population. He suggests that the industrialized nations must change their production and consumption patterns to use less natural resources and cause less pollution, adding that development in poor countries must be planned to eliminate poverty, meet basic human needs, and to protect the environment. He notes that population growth must be slowed to allow sustainable development because poverty, overpopulation, and underdevelopment are all interlinked. The fastest population growth is burdening the poorest nations, which are least able to meet the needs of new births and to invest in their future. Brundtland concludes that the increasing numbers of people in poor countries are deteriorating the earth and creating permanent damage to the environment because they struggle to survive, and cannot be concerned with planning for a tomorrow that may never come. As a result, impoverished environments in turn lead to even greater poverty, and a vicious cycle is created.

Brundtland observes that any nation's main asset should be its population, lamenting, "But when that population grows too fast, it becomes a liability instead." He noted that a rapidly growing population stifles the best efforts to provide proper education, nutrition, health care and shelter, while the earning capacity of the labor force suffers, and problems are compounded as job opportunities don't keep pace with the numbers seeking jobs. As wages go down and poverty is exacerbated. He proposed enhancing the role of women to increased economic growth, reduced poverty, provide better child and family welfare, and to lower birth rates. He warns that if men avoid responsibility for their sexual habits, fertility, and health, and if they reject their parental obligations, it will be impossible to deal with population growth, and with sexually transmitted diseases, including AIDS.

Finkle observes that as more governments identify their "population problem" as rapid population growth, leaders of developing countries realize that the health of their societies is dependent on the ability to provide jobs, schools, housing, and health care for their citizens, all of which are made more difficult by rapid population growth. He proposes the need for reducing the rate of population growth in order to remove major obstacles to economic development. Just how the North proposes to limit, reduce, and reverse population growth in the South is unclear. One thing is certain, the economic policies that western nations have implemented in regards to almost all of the Third World, have served to reduce economic development, which has resulted in faster population growth, and the institutionalizing of a vicious cycle of poverty, starvation, disease, and illiteracy. And among the elite power circles in the First World, there continues to be serious leanings by intellectuals and political thinkers to blame the Third World's burgeoning population for the evils of the world, for planetary deterioration, and environmental pollution that, if not arrested and reversed, will eventually threaten the very existence of the human species. Some "experts" may even feel that Third World genocide is a benevolent policy.

The Environmental Impact Paradigm

Keyfitz believes that the real limit to global population growth isn't determined by such things as the availability of food, natural disasters, or wars, but instead by the number of people who can be supported by the biosphere without disrupting its sensitive balance. Mankind is but one species among many, each with a place in nature, and each threatened with destruction if it grows to the point where it destroys the very environment upon which its existence depends. He observes that humans must co-exist with the AIDS virus and Ebola in the same manner as man-induced imbalance, measles, malaria, and other diseases, warning that human activities must not interfere with the inanimate aspects of the Earth that are essential for his existence, such as the ozone layer that provides protection from carcinogenic rays from space. He questions whether humans have the will to make sacrifices now, to protect the planet for future generations against the terrible consequences that may result from excessive human population, which he terms "an unstoppable collapse that follows from irreversible changes of which there are plentiful examples in the past."

Environmentalists see the planet's condition today at risk in the face of the far reaching, and unprecedented changes that the human population and its activities are now causing. Global warming is one such major concern, for example, as average air temperature in Denmark has increased 1.75 degrees Centigrade in 125 years from 1875 to 2000. If this rate of global warming continues, the ice caps will gradually melt, causing the flooding of coastal towns and cities, and in some cases reducing entire nation-states into nonexistence. By the year 2100, as compared to 1990 levels, greater demand will cause dramatic increases in the production of energy from all sources, including; a 50 percent increase in fossil fuel, a doubling of biomass, a quadrupling of hydroelectricity, a nine-fold jump in nuclear energy, and a twelve-fold expansion in renewable energy technologies. This will cause atmospheric CO_2 concentration in 2100 to increase from 355 ppm to a likely 500 ppm, a 40 percent increase from 1990 levels.

Grant provides additional global warming data, as an assessment confirmed a rise of between 0.3 deg. C to 0.6 deg. C in global mean surface temperature in the past century, and a related rise in global sea level of 10 to 25 cm. These rates will result in a temperature increase of 1.0 deg. to 3.5 deg. C by 2100, which is far faster than any warming trend in the Earth's past 10,000 years. Global warming will cause a rise of 15 –95 cm in average sea level by 2100, and the changes in both temperature and sea levels will continue in the centuries beyond 2100 *even if greenhouse gas concentrations are stabilized at current levels.* He further predicts that a complete melting of the Antarctic and Greenland ice caps would raise sea levels about 70 to 100 meters. Grant concludes that to avoid the greenhouse effect scenario that is primarily caused by human activities, a human population of perhaps 2 or 3 billion could be sustained at a decent level, commenting that this suggestion is less radical than it sounds, as it is where we were two generations ago (circa 1950).

On the other hand, Cohen pointes to a theoretical projection of global population to the year 2150 (similar to that prepared by the United Nations, 1992) that assumes regional levels of fertility are constant at 1950 levels, while life expectancy increases; the calculated population of 694 billion in 2150 could not be fed with conventional agriculture and water sources because annual global rainfall would be insufficient to grow the crops required for food. The renewable freshwater supply of the Earth is too limited for sustained agricultural irrigation and fertility, even if every drop of the 110,000 cubic kilometers of annual rain falling on land were used domestically for agriculture, and if people ate only 2,350 calories per day, the estimates of the maximum theoretical population that could be supported on Earth would range from 82 billion to 369 billion.

Keyfitz brings forth an ethical dilemma by questioning what share of the remainder of our planet's capacity to absorb emissions is the First World entitled to, as compared to the claims of the Third World. How legitimate is the South's position if they fail to reduce population growth? While the North has for decades restrained its population to less than two children per couple, can the South realistically expect the same material standard of living when their families are producing three, four or more children per couple? How will the First World arbitrate the its claims the need to preserve resources for future generations against those of the present, while competing with the Third World for as much of the world's resources as the North needs.

Abernethy adds that waste and deterioration of natural resources is likely a normal practice because private and local incentives to conserve is insufficient due to demand and disbelief in scarcity, as consumers believe they are better off without a commitment to share. It's often assumed that the great disparities in world living standards are due primarily to overpopulation in poor countries. Olson explains that given technology, fixed amounts of land and other natural resources, and level stocks of capital goods, increasing labor at some point yields diminishing productivity and also result in diminishing returns to nature's ability to absorb wastes.

In summary, the conventional wisdom of the First World that links population growth to potentially irreversible economic degradation is founded on four postulates:

1) The Earth's renewable resources, such as fresh water and aridable landmass for food production, are limited as in a zero-sum end game.

2) Population growth, particularly in the Third World, if unchecked, or even reversed, will lead to catastrophic and irreversible damage to our planet's ecosystem.

3) The First World's interest in self-propagation at a high standard of living is best served by limiting population growth in the Third World, preferably through strategies that limit or reverse their industrialization and population growth.

4) When increased human activities due to overpopulation impact the planet's closed biosphere to a point of diminished returns, great famines and disease will decimate the global population, primarily concentrated in the Third World.

Each of these First World assumptions shifting blame primarily to Third World population growth in not only self serving, but erroneous in its very premises, which will be discussed later in this journal's summary. The First World has historically, routinely, and systematically implements policies that result in the degradation, reduction, and genocide against dark-skinned peoples, in particular the black race. The North characterizes itself by eloquent statements in support of human rights, but a closer examination of western history discloses a sinister methodology of speaking "in the name of" some apparent humanitarian principle, only later to act "in spite of" the very principles they espouse. In the name of Christian brotherhood, the wars fought during the (un)Holy Crusades killed hundreds of thousands of "pagans", in order to save their souls, no doubt. In the name of "freedom" from supposed communist tyranny, the North killed millions of innocent women, men, and children as non-combatant "collateral" damage in South East Asia. Even Northern terminology is euphemistically and eloquently stated to reduce the appearance of its inhumane actions, by reducing the faces of those slaughtered into nomenclature only applicable to property, such as "collateral damage", as in damaged freight.

Nagengast defines political violence as overt state-sponsored or tolerated violence, which may or may not be direct violence. The violence between Hutus and Tutsi in Rwanda and Burundi; between Tamils and Sinhalese in Sri Lanka; between Latinos and indigenous peoples in Guatemala; and among Croats, Serbs, and Muslims in the Balkans, is tolerated or encouraged by states to create, justify, excuse, explain, or enforce disparate hierarchies and inequalities. These are incidents of state violence; and even though states may not appear on the surface to be primary agents, the deliberate acts of agents of the state cause mass starvation and similar economic or political misdeeds that result in widespread deaths, and even genocide. Lubeck described the scale of crisis in Africa gives it no option but to rely on a "reformed state" to regulate activity; consequently, chaos, starvation, and disintegration of states through neocolonial structures will follow as neo-liberal policies are strictly enforced. He adds that without debt relief and concessionary grants, Africa's primary commodity exporters can never hope to pay off their external debts (i.e. 350% of GDP), no matter how many neoliberal reforms are instituted internally.

Even in the most developed nation in the world, Peterson notes that a poverty paradox is one manifestation of a general deterioration in American society and culture where the spreading of an underclass culture (primarily blacks) is "undermining" the country's productive capacity, family life, social integration, and, ultimately its political stability. Petersen remarks, "Those underclass groups, American blacks being the extreme case, were compelled to come to or were forcefully incorporated into the United States and, once there, were subjected to poverty, discrimination, and slavery, constructed for themselves a conflictual understanding of the country's social and political institutions as the product of class dominance, racial prejudice and discrimination, cultural exclusiveness, over which they had little control." Grimes stated that draft regulations of the 60s and 70s ensured that most of those sent Vietnam were the poor and the Blacks. One desire of white supremacists has always been the fantasy of an all white country, resulting in genocide, Indian massacres, slavery, manifest destiny, Detroit, East St. Louis, Watts, the Mexican War.

Chinta Strausberg, writing in The "Chicago Defender", the oldest Black daily newspaper in America, warns Blacks must never forget the African Holocaust where more than 50 million lives were destroyed due to western greed for material wealth, further quoting Dr. James Small, a New York professor, who said:

"...these acts were crimes against humanity. All these people died because

someone was greedy and wasn't willing to work for it for themselves, so they forced other human beings to do it.... "And in the process, they took the lives of nearly 50 million men, women and children when we count those captured... killed on the ground in Africa, died in the dungeons waiting for slave ships from diseases and hunger, died in the middle passage coming to America in the time it took to get here in those slave ships and those that died on the plantations....Our life expectancy during the early part of slavery was not much more than five years, and they didn't mind working us to death because it was easy to replenish us. "In that 500-year period, we lost almost 50 million people and there are those who want us to forget it like it never happened.... Every effort was made by the enslavers to take away and to deny the humanity of the African. They were treated as objects, less than human. The Europeans used us as if we were their property. When we talk about killing the African spirit, it refers to the intent of white supremacy the dehumanization of African people by enslavement.

Hall reported that attached to the crime against humanity of enslavement was deprivation of liberty, forced labor, reduction of people into servitude, and trafficking in persons, particular women and children. Yates observed that humans destroy most species by destroying their habitats, rather than simply by killing them. Habitat destruction is a phenomenon rapidly occurring in the Third World, especially in Africa. Commenting on the plight of Africa, the Chinese U.N. Delegation stated "... colonialists and imperialists subjected... Africa... to brutal aggression and enslavement... and have not only plundered enormous social wealth from... Africa, but also engaged in human trafficking and evicted or slaughtered local inhabitants. Africa alone has lost as many as 100 million people in this way... the social productive forces in... African... countries were seriously sapped. The North has a long history of exploiting, enslaving, impoverishing and killing Blacks.

The United States of America hegemon, while marketing itself to the world as the defender of human rights, actually provides a platform that initiates, supports, and implements global genocide through surrogates and Third World agents. LaRouche reports a public declaration in the September 1946 edition of "The Bulletin of the Atomic Scientists", made by Bertran Russell, "who was emphatic in stating that he was promoting nuclear weapons for no other purpose but establishing world government. Russell insisted, then, and later, that the U.S.A. and Britain should prepare to bomb the Soviet Union with nuclear weapons, for the contingency that Soviet General Secretary Josef Stalin might refuse to submit to transforming the United Nations Organization into an actual world government, thus eliminating the sovereignties of all of the world's nation-states."

Grimes observes that in Vietnam, the myth of America as liberator was in danger of collapse because during the Vietnam War, it was evident that American military forces was not liberating anyone, but was slashing blindly through the Vietnamese landscape murdering anyone, regardless of political persuasion. Singer argues that the largeness of current populations is not needed for progressive development or the maintenance of diversity, adding that if blunders result in a nuclear war, and thereby eliminate nine-tenths of the human lives on our planet, the scattered survivors would find themselves with the "appropriate" phenotype to enable a "wiser fresh start."

The U.S., long a supporter of war crimes trials for crimes against humanity, such as genocide, instead attempts to exempt itself from the legal jurisdiction of international courts to avoid the surrender of Americans. The chances that the United States will be able to win the exemption of Americans from the court's jurisdiction are diminishing rapidly. Consequently, political choices in the Third World often appear to be determined by taking positions contrary to those of the United States, based on a simplistic syllogism:

1.   The United States advises a particular policy.

2.   Any advice of the United States corresponds to its own interests and might be, or is likely contrary to our interests.

3.   Conclusion: We should reject American policies.

The structural components of violence and power as facets of First World hegemonism, and its projection through economic, cultural, and political imperialism, colonialism, and neocolonialism into the Third World. Utilizing various pseudo-intellectual justifications such as "racial superiority", "overpopulation", and "environmental deterioration", the North has implemented military and economic strategies to subjugate, exploit, and degrade the states and people of the South. The increasing alarm over an expanding world population, predominantly in the Third World, is in large part motivated by a western paranoia of both becoming overrun by non-white people, and a potential threat to human existence due to the possible exhaustion of natural resources required for survival. This notion of "race suicide" compels the North to consider and devise self-propagation scenarios and strategies that act to the detriment of developing and underdeveloped states, up to and including genocide.

As a result of First World fears, avarice, and immorality, Pope John Paul II noted that broad segments of public opinion justify certain crimes against life in the name of individual freedoms and rights. The emergence of a "veritable culture of death" is fostered by powerful cultural, economic and political forces which encourage society to be overly concerned with efficiency. Consequently, from this point of view, the world has become in a certain sense, a war of the powerful against the weak. The Pope adds, "On a more general level, there exists in contemporary culture a certain Promethean attitude which leads people to think that they can control life and death by taking the decisions about them into their own hands. We see a tragic expression of all this in the spread of euthanasia, disguised and surreptitious or practiced openly and even legally... is sometimes justified by the utilitarian motive of avoiding costs which bring no return and which weight heavily on society. Thus it is proposed to eliminate malformed babies, the severely handicapped, the disabled, the elderly, especially when they are not self-sufficient, and the terminally ill. Nor can we remain silent in the face of other more furtive, but no less serious and real forms of euthanasia... Today not a few of the powerful of the earth are haunted by the current demographic growth and fear that the most prolific and poorest peoples represent a threat for the well-being and peace of their own countries.

The proposed American "National Missile Defense" (NMD) system will permit the unchallenged projection of First World nuclear and economic power against the Third World. History has shown that the North routinely practices policies that ensure Euro-American global military, political, and economic dominance and control over world resources, to maintain their superior position utilizing policies that directly or indirectly result in the genocide of the world's non-white people, and destruction of Third World cultures, states, and regional economies.

How can Third World nations use the international forum to discredit the First World's recurring attempts to legitimize and justify genocidal policies as the ultimate solution to Third World overpopulation that purportedly threatens the quality and existence of human life on Earth? There are intermediary steps that must be taken to forestall the North's use of weapons of mass destruction as a population control measure. First, the international community must agree to arrest population at current levels through sensible reproductive quotas and policies, and to reduce overall native populations over time. Couples must be limited to no more than two offspring, as a realistic population stabilization policy. This quota should result in an eventual drop in overall population due to an excessive rate of mortality from environmental causes and infant mortality over live births. In recent decades, China has made significant advances in developing their economy while successfully controlling population growth. The natural population growth rate dropped to 1.154 percent in 1983, from 2.089 percent in 1973, and the people's living standards have improved. The Chinese family planning and population controlled-growth policies, in tandem with planned economic development has been the correct model for China, and may be an effective model for the rest of the Third World.

Following China's example, the UN should encourage a global two live births per couple policy as a means to stabilize population, encourage a redistribution of excess First World resources to improve living standards and GDP, especially in less developed countries. Increasing the development and modernization of LDCs enhances global political and social stability that is a requisite for capital growth, which reinforces a cycle of increased modernization and development. Greater regional, common-market, and global commons trade should "raise the tide for all ships, large and small". It is likely the paradigm of uneven distribution of global resources from poor nations to the rich will continue, but First World nations know only too well that increasing economic development of LDCs will likely result in decreasing world population through peaceful, rather than traditional violent means. Grant (205) weighs in on population policy, insisting parents need have no more than two children to carry on their family, and while it was once necessary to have many children so that some might survive to maturity, that is no longer true in most parts of the world.

While every living being has a natural urge and right to reproduce, even in nature, excessive numbers of any species eventually lead to catastrophic suffering and mortality. In order to avert a mass mortality scenario for human beings, sensible international agreements and political policies must be made. China's one birth per couple policy is a sensible effort to decrease that nations population through non-violent means. Depending upon overall population demographics, international benchmarks might become necessary, such that nations with populations over 300 million must actualize a 1.5 live births per couple quota (as expressed by 3 live births per every two couples, utilizing a lottery system). Similarly, nations with 500 million or more populations must agree to a 1.25 births per couple quota. Nations with 1 billion or more population must agree to 1 birth per couple quota.

Only through implementing proactive non-violent population control strategies, coupled with improving non-polluting technologies, and providing capital incentives for political and social stabilization, will the First World lose its temptation to make genocidal "first strikes" against the developing world. History has shown that the First World hegemon will not do anything that is against its self-interests. Consequently, LDCs must take steps to negotiate strategies that will encourage First World capital investment in exchange for population control, returning a reasonable "Return On Investment" to the First World. The North owns and exploits over 80 percent of the world's non-renewable resources, consequently, it must restrain its avarice, and recognize its responsibility to redistribute at least a small percentage of excessive wealth, and restrict its consumption of world resources to no more than current levels. The First World must act morally and responsibly to restrain its temptation to project violence. The First World must practice what it preaches, act as the champion of human rights which its philosophical and legal tenets profess. If the First World assists the development of LCDs in exchange for non-violent population control measures, the tide will rise for all humanity as biosphere destruction is arrested. But how likely are the First World elites and LCDs likely to adopt such rational approaches to the zero-sum game of population control and environmental protection? History and current environmental scans suggests a mixed and uncertain future.

Blands (25-26) stated that it required 35 years from1965 for 3.3 B people to doubled in 2000 to 6.5 B people, a population that is inadequately fed by the cultivation of 56 percent of the world's arable land. If agricultural productivity in the less developed countries could be raised to that in the United States, there would be an enormous increase in agricultural output. By increasing the existing levels of agricultural production, as well as the potential for increasing the amount of land under cultivation, he found that the "potential gross cropped area would then be sufficient for

38-48 billion people, or 10-13 times the present human population of the earth. If these projections are reasonably accurate, it appears the world can still accommodate limited human population growth beyond the current 6.2 B people to 38 B, limited by arable land, or 82 B from natural rainfall limits.

Clinton warns that a population strategy targeting Third World birth rates could be taken as a form of repression, as a preventive form of class and racial genocide, and if all of population policy focused on limiting births, based on perceived upper limits of supportable birth rates, this would equate to a genocidal act of the rich against the poor, the white against the colored races, and the West against the East. Boot opines, "The global social structure is based on selfishness, maintained by power-play, marred by short-run vision, and managed by crisis-hopping. The rich, while luxuriating in wealth, pay lip-service to serious problems shared by all, but lack inclination to act decisively. In the back of their minds they surely believe in the survival of the fittest. They are the fittest. The poor, distrustful of the rich, are so burdened with short-run survival that the long-run problems seem insignificant."

Finnln discloses that "it requires about one-third of the world's annual extraction of nonrenewable resources to support the 6 percent of the world's population in the United States at the per capita level to which it is thought the rest of the world should become accustomed." He estimates that if U.S. levels of technology could prevail worldwide, current resources could support no more than 18 percent of the world's population at U.S. levels, with nothing left over for the remainder 82 percent. Paradoxically, without the labor services of the lower 82 percent, the rich 18 percent would not be as rich as they might think.

Keohane summarizes the international predicament by stating, "The sources of hegemony therefore include sufficient military power to deter or rebuff attempts to capture and close off important areas of the world political economy. But in the contemporary world, at any rate, it is difficult for a hegemon to use military power directly to attain its economic policy objectives with its military partners and allies." He adds, "Hegemons require deference to enable them to construct a structure of world capitalist order. It is too expensive, and perhaps self-defeating, to achieve this by force; after all, the key distinction between hegemony and imperialism is that a hegemon, unlike an empire, does not dominate societies through a cumbersome political superstructure, but rather supervises the relationships between politically independent societies through a combination of hierarchies of control and the operation of markets. Hegemony rests on the subjective awareness by elites in secondary states that they are benefiting...."

In conclusion, a united international community can make inroads to resist and eventually change First World hegemonic paranoia by debunking the legitimacy of long held pseudo-scientific theories on the causes of poverty, population growth, ecological degradation, and economic-political competition in the perceived zero-sum end game from consumption of world resources.

1)   The Earth's resources are relatively untapped. Our deepest wells barely scratch the Earth's crust, and cheaper technology can be developed to increase global storage and supplies of fresh water (desalinization, etc.), as biotechnology continues to improve crop yields and the arability of land. Technology can also be called upon to restore the arability of top soil in non-productive regions, and top soil erosion can be

ameliorated by digging into the crust to access the rich minerals contained in the Earth's mantle, as in volcanic magma. The rich resources of Africa and many areas of the world are essentially untapped, but these areas must not be exploited to the detriment of its native populations, who should instead be the beneficiaries of development. By removing the erroneous presumption that resource consumption is non-renewable and non-recyclable, the world can reject the notion of limits in a zero-sum end game, and begin to search for new sources of abundance located deeper in the crust, in volcanoes, geysers, and in the Earth's deep oceans and mantle. Alternative energy sources, based on discoveries in new quantum physics that can generate electricity and motion by harnessing strong gravitational forces, near frictionless materials, and electro-magnetic applications could be developed once "big oil interests" are politically reduced, as new technologies replace the need for burning fossil fuels for energy.

2)   Population growth, particularly in the Third World, would likely follow First World patterns of natural reduction that follows economic development, and the liberation of women from their roles as birthing machines. In the male dominated and chauvinistic world, men must take greater procreative responsibility, utilizing birth control methods to prevent child births when they are unable to afford the expense of childrearing. Having children simple to satisfy the egocentric desire to continue one's lineage is insufficient rationale for expecting women to give birth. Each child born into the world has a right, and deserves to have at a minimum, food, shelter, education, and love, with the goal of liberty and self-actualization. Again, technological breakthroughs stand to assist family planning efforts, through reversible sterilization, surrogate

birthing utilizing xeno-placental techniques, and other strategies that emphasize responsible parenting choices. Overbeek (191) explores the possibility of adding contraceptive agents to certain foods, providing another drug to neutralize the sterilizing effects of the contraceptive agent for those who desire pregnancy. If it were added to certain foods only, then only those wanting to be sterile could consume those foods.

The First World's self-propagation at a high standard of living can best be assured by global partnership, and not wanton exploitation of the Third World. The waste that exist in the North alone, is more than sufficient to maintain the developing world, consequently, conservation in the First World allows the South to improve its economies, and through non-pollution strategies, both West and the East can become responsible partners to, and not abusers of our planet. The traditional "competition" paradigm must necessarily be replaced by a "partnership" paradigm.

3)   Human activities due to population growth need not have a negative impact on the planet's closed   biosphere. A point of diminishing returns can be avoided if popular awareness drives a consistent motivation to conserve and respect the planet and its resources that gives humans life. As long as the First World has more incentives to partnership with the Third World, there will be less pressure for hegemonic exploitation and oppression of the poor. The world's monetary systems have for several decades been de-linked from the "gold standard." Many foreign currencies are linked to the stability of the U.S. Dollar. In reality, world trade flows between computers that track 1's and 0's, as the ledger between debits and credits. The strength of the world economy is in large part dependent on domestic and global confidence in the First

World's (particularly the U.S.) ability to honor its currencies in exchange for technology, manufactured goods, and military assistance. In the hierarchy of the technological and commodities "food chain", the world's economy would collapse if the masses lost confidence in the purchasing value of western capital to buy "big ticket" items, such as ships, planes, tanks, manufacturing plants, and commercial computer systems, in addition to massive quantities of food and medicines that the west produces. The logical expectation is when a state's currency is honored for large top end items, it most certainly will support the daily purchases required to sustain comfortable lives.

The North must remove the blinders of its avarice, and realize that the rest of the world depends in large part on the First World's economic vitality and humane leadership. The Third World has little desire to threaten (nor is it capable of such) the West, and instead desires to partnership with it, rather than to be its victim. Gradually raising the economic tide of the world over a generation can solve most of persistent global problems, and offers a greater opportunity for sustained peace. The world economic paradigm must necessarily change from one of competition and exploitation to one of partnership and exchange. Only then will the peoples and governments of the world realize sustained and effective cooperation to reduce population growth, and the negative impact of humans on the global environment; therefore providing a realistic platform for human progress and evolution while safeguarding the planetary ecosystem for future generations.

The First World hegemon, occupying the superior power position, can show greater wisdom beyond its greed, and take proactive steps to harness the abundance of our planet, rather than to view the world through the prejudicial and reality distorting filters of gloom and doom. It is the North that currently possesses the resources, capital, and technology to take the world *beyond conflict, violence, and war.* The orthodox zero-sum game paradigm is ruining the planet, nations, and directly or indirectly results in the genocide of Third World peoples. The question is, what will it take for the hegemon to adjust its operative policies and philosophical constructs to permit it to view the world and its great diversity in a more realistic and positive framework? The bottom line is whether or not the violent prone First World hegemon has the desire and will to bring true human rights to the world stage, beyond political rhetoric and positioning for selfish gains. The hopes of the world's population depend on a constructive reorientation of the North's role in the global community, from one of foe, to that of friend, and if the First World can see that's in its own interest, anything is possible. Conflict, violence, war, and extinction is not inevitable or certain.

References

Abernethy, Virginia, "Comment: The 'One World' Thesis as an Obstacle to Environmental Preservation," *Population and Development Review*, Vol. 16, Issue Supplement; "Resources, Environment, and Population: Present Knowledge, Future Options," (1990), 323-328.

Bland, Chester, and Dwight E. Lee, *Lectures in History* (Worcester, MA: Clark University Press, 1976).

Boot, John C. G., *Common Globe or Global Commons* (New York, NY: Marcel Dekker, 1974).

Brundtland, Gro Harlem, "Population, Environment, and Development." *Population and Development Review*, Vol. 19, Issue 4 (Dec., 1993), 893-899.

Chinese Delegation, "Chinese Statements on Population at Bucharest, 1974, and Mexico City, 1984." *Population and Development Review*, Vol. 20, Issue 2 (Jun., 1994), 449-459.

Clinton, Richard L., William S. Flash, and R. Kenneth Godwin, *Political Science in Population*

Cohen, Joel E., "Should Population Projections Consider 'Limiting Factors" - and If So, How?" *Population and Development Review*, Vol 24, Issue Supplement: "Frontiers of Population Forecasting" (1998), 118-138.

Finkle, Jasor L., and Alisen McIntosh, "The New Politics of Population," *Population and Development Review*, Vol 20, Issue Supplement: "The New Politics of Population: Conflict and Consensus in Family Planning" (1994), 3-34.

Finnin, William M. Jr., and Gerald Alonzo Smith, Editors, *The Morality of Scarcity, Limited Resources and Social Policy* (Baton Rouge, LA: Louisiana State University Press, 1979).

Gilland, Bernard, "World Population, Economic Growth, and Energy Demand, 1990-2100: A Review of Projections," *Population and Development Review*, Vol. 21, Issue 3 (Sep., 1995), 507-539.

Grant, Lindsey, *Juggernaut, Growth on a Finite Planet* (Santa Ana, CA: Seven Locks Press, 1996)

Grimes, Kyle, "The Entropics of Discourse: Michael Harper's Debridement and the Myth of the Hero," *Black American Literature Forum*, Vol. 24, No. 3 (Autumn, 1990), pp. 417-440.

Hall, Christopher K., "The First Five Sessions of the UN Preparatory Commission for the International Criminal Court," *American Journal of International Law*, Vol. 94, No. 4 (Oct., 2000), pp. 773-789.

Hodgson, Dennis, "The Ideological Origins of the Population Association of America," *Population and Development Review*, Vol. 17, Issue 1 (Mar., 1991), 1-34.

Kasarda, John D., and Edward M. Crenshaw, "Third World Urbanization: Dimensions, Theories, and Determinants," *Annual Review of Sociology*, Vol. 17 (1991), 467-501.

Keohane, Robert O., "Hegemony in the World Political Economy," Reprinted by Permission in *International Politics*, 5 Edition, by Art, Robert J., and Robert Jervis, (New York, NY: Addison Wesley Longman, 2000).

Keyfitz, Nathan, "Population Growth, Development and the Environment," *Population Studies*, Vol. 50, Issue 3 (Nov., 1996), 335-359.

Keyfitz, Nathan, "Toward a Theory of Population-Development Interactions," *Population and Development Review*, Vol 16, Issue Supplement: "Resources, Environment, and Population: Present Knowledge, Future Options" (1990), 295-314.

Kremer, Michael Kremer, "Population Growth and Technological Change: One Million B.C. to 1990," *Quarterly Journal of Economics*, Volume 108, Issue 3 (Aug., 1993), 681-716.

LaRouche, Lyndon H. Jr., *Now, Are You Ready To Learn Economics?* (Washington D.C.: EIR News Service, Inc., 2000).

LaRouche, Lyndon H. Jr., *The Road To Recovery* (Leesburg, VA: New Bretton Woods, 1999).

Lubeck, Paul M., "The Crisis of African Development: Conflicting Interpretations and Resolution," *Annual Review of Sociology*, Vol. 18 (1992), 519-540.

Malkki, Liisa H., "Refugees and Exile: From "Refugee Studies" to the National Order of Things," *Annual Review of Anthropology*, Vol. 24 (1995), pp. 495-523.

McGeveran, William A. Jr., Ed., *The World Almanac and Book of Facts* 2001, (Mahwah, N.J.: World Almanac Books, 2001), pp. 372, 860.

Nagengast, Carole, "Violence, Terror, and the Crisis of the State," *Annual Review of Anthropology*, Vol. 23 (1994), pp. 109-136.

Neuhouser, Frederick, "Freedom, Dependency, and the General Will," *The Philosophical Review*, Volume 102, Issue 3 (Jul. 1993), pg. 363-395.

Olson, Mancur, "Mancur Olson on the Key to Economic Development," *Population and Development Review*, Vol. 24, Issue 2 (Jun., 1998), 369-379.

Olson, Mancur Jr., "Distinguished Lecture on Economics in Government: Big Bills Left on the Sidewalk: Why Some Nations are Rich, and Others Poor," *The Journal of Economic Perspectives*, Vol. 10, Issue 2 (Spring, 1996), 3-24.

Overbeek, Johannes, *The Population Challenge* (London, England: Greenwood Press, 1976).

Pasqualucci, Paolo, "Hobbes and the Myth of 'Final War.'" *Journal of the History of Ideas*, Vol. 51, Issue 4 (Oct.-Dec., 1990), 647-657.

Peterson, Paul E., "The Urban Underclass and the Poverty Paradox," *Political Science Quarterly*, Vol. 106, Issue 4 (Winter, 1991). (Peterson, 623)

Pope John Paul II, "Abortion, Contraception, and Euthanasia," *Population and Development Review*, Vol. 21, Issue 3 (Sep., 1995), 689-696.

Scott, John T., "The Theodicy of the Second Discourse: The 'Pure State of Nature' and Rousseau's Political Thought," *The American Political Science Review*, Volume 86, Issue 3 (Sep. 1992), pp. 696-711.

Shuger, Debora, "Irishmen, Aristocrats, and Other White Barbarians," *Renaissance Quarterly*, Vol. 50, No. 2 (Summer, 1997), pp. 494-525.

Singer, S. Fred, Editor, *Is There an Optimum Level of Population?* (N.Y.: McGraw-Hill, 1971)

Smith, Estellie M., "The Process of Sociocultural Continuity," *Current Anthropology*, Vol. 23, No. 2 (Apr., 1982), pp. 127-142.

Tapinos, Georges, and Phyllis T. Piotrow, *Six Billion People* (N.Y., NY: McGraw-Hill, 1978).

Waltz, Kenneth N., "The Anarchic Structure of World Politics,"
Reprinted with permission in *International Politics*, 5th Edition by Robert J.
Art and Robert Jervis, (New York, NY: Addison Wesley Longman, 2000),
pp. 49-51.

Weller, Robert H., and Leon F. Bouvier, *Population Demography and Policy* (New York, NY: St. Martin's Press, 1981).

Wilmoth, John, and Patrick Bal, "The Population Debate in American Popular Magazines, 1946-90." *Population and Development Review*, Vol. 18, Issue 4 (Dec., 1992), 631-668.

Yates, Wilson, *Family Planning on a Crowded Planet* (Minneapolis, Minnesota: Augugsburg Publishing House, 1971).

Oprah became a billionaire by relating to middle-class white women

Chapter 4 – Is there an end racism?

The world system and global economic order based on a bifurcated capitalistic system where the top ten percent of people own and/or control 80% of global resources creates and reinforces many inequities that result in the preventable suffering and deaths of millions of innocent people each year. It would be more beneficial for all classes and races of people were the rich and powerful to understand that providing abundance to all people regardless of race, class, nationality and regionalism create ample opportunities to magnify the existing wealth of the elites many folds as the rising tide lifts all boats.

Furthermore, as technology and more efficient techniques are developed to farm the world's minerals and natural resources, replacing deforestation, water pollution, fossil fuels with new terra farming, harnessing the oceans and wave motions, lightening collection farming, more efficient wind and solar energy, more energy efficient vehicles and appliance, and improved methods for water conservation and desalinization, there should be no reason anyone in the world must be underfed, denied adequate medical care, or allowing able bodied people to work in newly spawned industries that robots haven't taken over.

Conspiracy theorists have promoted New World Order scenarios for the past decade, concluding that globalization, the rise of oligarchies, and the computer-technology explosion are the means through which the singular world government will come about. Juxtaposed against the one world order paradigm is American hegemony and military might, as the sole remaining "superpower" in the world.

Let's examine the logic, evidence and motivation behind the creation of a singular world government. Let's explore the probable answers to the essential questions that must be resolved before credibility should be attributed to the global empire paradigm. The answer to these questions will greatly clarify the potential effects of globalization, as a means toward creating a centralized world government.

1.   Why would any individual, group, nation, or ethnic group desire to rule the world, with all of its problems, conflicts and turmoil? What are historical precedents and reasons for empire building and world domination?

2.   If it were possible for any one individual, group, race, ethnicity, or nation to rule the world, how could they accomplish such an enormous and complex feat?

3.   What individuals, groups, or nations could have the desire to rule the world? Who might they be, why, and why during our modern era?

4.   What individuals, groups, or nations actually possess the potential resources, economic, political and military power that would be required to rule the world?

5.   Of those with such awesome potential power, desire and capability, which individuals, groups, or national leaders would most likely be the ones to attempt world domination and world rule?

6.   What obstacles could prevent the creation of a singular world ruler or government?

7.   What aspects of a centralized world government could be beneficial to humanity, which aspects would be destructive, and in what ways?

8.   How could the power of a centralized world government be abused?

9.   What international safeguards can be put in place to prevent abuse of global economic, political, and military power?

10.   What technological safeguards should be put in place to prevent global thermal nuclear war, or limited nuclear war, should a singular world ruler or government eventually have dominion over all the nations of the world?

Ethical bureaucracy as a safeguard against racism

Improving the quality of public servants is an issue that is gaining greater public and political awareness. Is the public interest best served by those who are motivated to draw on their government experience and stature for private gain? Stark opined that the public is not best served by officials who, are motivated to spend more time working on certain files, cultivating certain kinds of contacts, and devote more energy to acquiring certain kind of reputation, than they would were they less concerned to use their time in office to develop marketable skills and capacities (Stark, 1997).

Contributing to the temptation for some in public service to enhance their own marketability is the lure of post-public employment opportunities created by the push to reinvent government by adopting "new public management" strategies such as privatization. Durant raises fundamental questions on the basic premise of private sector superiority to deliver public services.... But are market-based approaches to service delivery do more with less, more effectively, and in the public interest than did government bureaucracies prior to privatization? Or do they as critics claim, only produce the worst of both worlds, leading to lower efficiency, quality, employee security, and public accountability? (Durant, 1998).

The push to balance government budgets at all levels has contributed to a retrenchment from public service. Wilson (1996) opined that, "as spending on social programs decreases, the growth of joblessness and welfare receipt mainly reflect a declining commitment to the core values of society" (Wilson, 1996). Many public officials have become frustrated by the apparent inability of the legislative process to accommodate non-partisan views, as indicated by a significant number who leave the House of Representatives because they didn't feel the structure allowed them to promote policies they personally support (Moore, 1998). While some politicians lose their spirit of public service, and are either voted out, or voluntarily resign, the bureaucracy provides ample opportunity for the exercise of individual judgment and policy-making. Coleman (1998) describes the dilemma of bureaucratic decision-making authority:

The delegation of policy-making authority to the administrative agencies of government poses a fundamental dilemma in democratic societies. On the one hand, administrative discretion is essential since legislators can not anticipate all of the possible circumstances that may arise in the applications of public laws. As a result, bureaucrats are asked to draw upon their experience, expertise, judgment, and intuition to make administrative decisions. But on the other hand, public administrators lack accountability at the ballot box, and civil service regulations designed to prevent political manipulation shield them from elected officials, as their specialization, expertise, and clientele support constrain the ability of political officials to control bureaucratic action (Coleman, 1998).

It is ironic that many elected officials called upon to represent "the people" lose their desire to serve the public, from frustration or desire to profit from their public service repertoire and connections by hiring on with the private sector. Both politicians and bureaucrats have often become manipulators of public sentiment, rather than sincerely serving the public good. Often, simply by coining new words, or by eloquent but confusing explanations of intent, public servants are able to present their personal slant on public service, under the guise of public benefit. Chabot (1995) referred to Montaigne, a Thomas Hobbes contemporary, who opined that euphemisms of language "could any longer evaluate the fairness of its conduct or the sincerity of its motives. Viciousness donned the cloak of righteousness. Ambition had become courage, stubbornness masquerading as piety, and behind every diplomatic overture there lurked a blasphemous heart (Chabot, 1995). It is unlikely that the sincere spirit of public service exemplified by the lives of public spirited individuals such as Perkins, Delany, and Adams would allow the degradation of the public good, without issuing vehement social and political protest and sacrificing their lives to positive social and political change.

A review of biographical and historical material, scholars' views, case studies, and philosophical aspects of public service provides a rich tapestry of diversity and individualism focused on benefiting the greater common good. If we see a future vision of prosperity, cooperation, and humanity, we will likely achieve it. If we see a future of chaos and warfare, we will probably focus our limited resources on preparing for the next war, and perhaps even the "final war" to end all wars, the one that might bring the end to human existence. What societies collectively view as probable future scenarios is what human beings are likely to receive, if for no other reason than the self-filling prophecy. Political leaders need to describe a clearer vision of the type of future that humans need, want, and are capable of achieving.

If unregulated capitalism is allowed to reinforce and advance highly disparate realities between the rich and the poor, instead of becoming a positive driving force for advancing all human beings while preserving the global environment, then we can expect more accelerated outcomes that lead to greater degrees of conflict, violence, and war. The universal purpose of wealth building should be to fulfill humanitarian missions that provide improvements to service human needs in health care, education, infrastructure, environment, science, arts, music, space exploration, and elevating the human spirit, morals and civility. Media and marketing should change their focus from creating illusions that create artificial needs like cosmetics, to public service that addresses the real needs of people, such as health care, food, and shelter.

Why can't media and business promote new worthwhile competitive "sports" that include equal access and contributions of both men and women on the same teams, where something productive is accomplished besides placing another ball through another hole. How about teams who compete to build the best houses in the shortest period of time, or who clean a mile of beach front in the fastest time? Why not propose a game where children are taught new skills, then compete to demonstrate their competence in applying those skills, for example in designing and building a simple robot? In this way, we can elevate the desirability of accomplishing things that benefit the public good, and are not simply escapist activities that benefit the relatively few professional team owners or competitors.

Unfortunately, human civilizations have been mired in exploiting the masculine dominance paradigm at the great disadvantage of females and societies in general. Gender insecurities are reinforced by media advertising to create markets for clothes, cars, cosmetics, and "crappy" products, where buying "name brands" translates to higher profits with little or no appreciable value added for consumers. Why not create genderless markets that instill the love of community, environment, and public service, where all interested people could participate, regardless of sex, race, age, disability, ethnicity, culture or religion? Do we really need another "awards" show to celebrate "celebrities"? How about awards shows that celebrate the best that each occupation has produced; the best teachers, carpenters, fishers, farmers, police, parents, and so on?

Until societies can celebrate reality instead of illusions, then our combined destinies will likely remain stuck on superficialities while the real problems of the world continue to be ignored, compounded, and exacerbated until perhaps it's too late. The spirit of public service demands that leadership, resources, and public awareness be focused on dealing with reality, and not in illusory escapism from the real world. When the capitalism paradigm shifts from profiting on illusion creation and fulfillment, to profiting from real world problems resolution, then humans will witness their greatest period of advancement, far beyond what even the Renaissance Period had produced.

Let the spirit of public service push us forward into an era of peace and enlightenment, and away from the dismal dichotomy of global exploitation of the poor, females, and color peoples. Let the spirit of public service build better and more civil societies for all. I believe that an engaged citizen is one who loves his nation and cherishes his family and community, and demonstrates desire to improve life for others. Americans are the global leaders by default, for good and for bad, and it behooves our leaders and residents to try to improve the conditions of our nation and the world.

Biographies of great achievers and leaders indicate that a prerequisite of vision, powerful connections, public support, and persistence set apart the enduring "doers" from the lot. History also has shown that the social and political climate must be ripe for change, in order for positive change to occur. The world may be within such an opportune moment in evolving history, to seize the momentum to push for rapid positive changes through the cooperation and support of elite capitalists and political leaders to push for a kinder, gentler, more responsible, and more humanitarian and environmentally sensible form of capitalism. Society needs desperately to change cultural socialization to eliminate concepts that cause inequality, exploitation, and violence, thereby creating a more civil society. Thirdly, public service is called upon to create environments where every human being can pursue happiness through appropriate infrastructure support, institutional equity, structural fairness, and the exercise of personal conscience to do what's right and in the best interest of the public good.

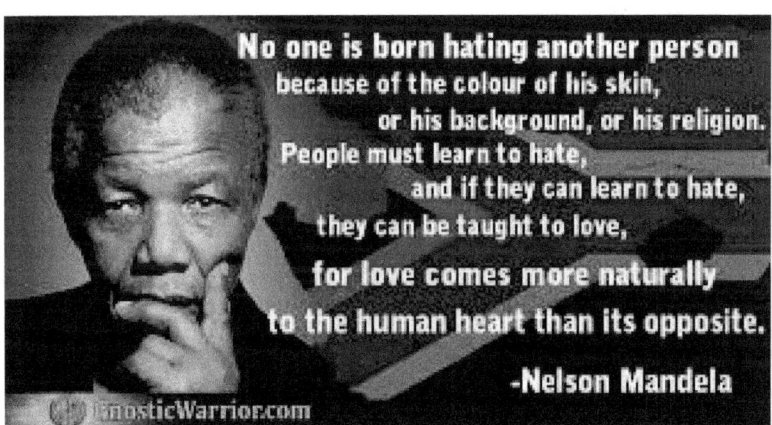

No one is born hating another person because of the colour of his skin, or his background, or his religion. People must learn to hate, and if they can learn to hate, they can be taught to love, for love comes more naturally to the human heart than its opposite.

-Nelson Mandela

GnosticWarrior.com

Human beings can make the world a better place, except that it will required the leadership and support of elite actors. The "zero-sum game" paradigm continues to dictate perceptual reality and the distorted paradigms upon which most socialized people based their beliefs and actions. Social construction has created a set of mirrors that provides a distorted view of reality, and until global leaders choose to look beyond their insular biases, and view the human race and planet Earth as one interrelated biosphere, then little change can take place. The world is what the human collective makes it, for better or for worse. People who justify the exploitation of others through dishonesty and corruption may obtain substantial material and monetary gains during their lifetimes, but the cost to the human species is likely to be paid by future generations whose survival may be jeopardized by the unethical behavior and strategies of greedy people in the present.

References

Chabot, Dana, 1995. "Thomas Hobbes: skeptical moralist", *The American Political Science Review*, Vol. 89, Issue 2 (June, 1995), 401-410. Retrieved from the World Wide Web, March 1, 2002 from http://www.jstor.org.

Coleman, Sally, Jeffrey L. Brucney, and J. Edward Kellough, 1998. "Bureaucracy as a representative institution; toward a reconciliation of bureaucratic government and democratic theory", *American Journal of Political Science*, Vol. 42, Issue 3 (July, 1998), 717-744. Retrieved from the World Wide Web, March 1, 2002 from **http://www.jstor.org**.

Durant, Robert F., Jerome S. Legge Jr., and Antony Moussios, "People, profits, and service delivery: lessons from the privatization of British Telecom", *American Journal of Political Science*, Vol. 42, Issue 1 (Jan, 1998), 117-140. Retrieved from the World Wide Web, March 1, 2002 from http://www.jstor.org.

Moore, Michael K., and John R. Libbing, 1998. "Situational dissatisfaction in Congress:explaining voluntary departures", *The Journal of Politics*, Vol. 60, Issue 4 (Nov., 1998), 1083-1107. Retrieved from the World Wide Web, March 1, 2002 from http://www.jstor.org.

Neuhouser, Frederick. "Freedom, dependency, and the general will", *The PhilosophicalReview*, Volume 102, Issue 3 (Jul. 1993), pg. 363-395.

Ogunleye, Tolagbe, 1998. "Dr. Martin Robison Delany, 19th-Century Africana Womanists: reflections on his avant-garde politics concerning gender, colorism, and nation building", *Journal of Black Studies*, Vol. 28, Issue 5 (May, 1998), 628-649. Retrieved from the World Wide Web, March 1, 2002 from http://www.jstor.org.

Oskin, Becky, 2002. "St. Luke, Tenet sued by patients", *Pasadena Star-News*, Feb. 7, 2002.

Scott, John T. "The theodicy of the second discourse: the 'pure state of nature' and Rousseau's political thought", *The American Political Science Review*, Volume 86, Issue 3 (Sep. 1992), pgs. 696-711.

Stark, Andrew, 1997. "Beyond quid pro quo: what's wrong with private gain from public office?" *The American Political Science Review*, Vol. 91, Issue 1 (Mar., 1997), 108-120. Retrieved from the World Wide Web, March 1, 2002 from http://www.jstor.org.

Wilson, William J., 1996. "When work disappears", *Political Science Quarterly*, Vol. 111, Issue 4 (Winter 1996-1997), 567-595. Retrieved from the World Wide Web, March 1, 2002 from http://www.jstor.org.

Conclusions

The powerful elites in the West, backed by their mighty militaries and bio weapons research facilities with virtually unlimited monetary resources are likely to stay the path they've been on since the end of WWII. They will likely use all of their financial organizations, control of the global monetary markets, and multinational corporations to further exploit the resources of the Third World, and where indigenous non-white governments stand in the way, regime change is orchestrated. When the conventional wisdom is to cleanse the landscape of indigenous peoples to permit a more efficacious exploitation of natural resources, bio weapons are unleashed on the unsuspecting populations as a form of racial cleansing so puppet governments can be installed to oppress the survivors. That has been the historical operating strategy of the powerful elitist invaders.

The world of humanitarian idealism has pushed the world forward, only to slide back before reaching the goals. We live in an era of perpetual war, perpetual poverty, perpetual crime, perpetual corruption, and perpetual greed. And there's no end in sight unless the existing global economic structure is dismantled and abandoned in favor of an equitable value for value trade and monetary system based on simple interest rather than compound interest. The world worships GOD, gold, oil, and debt. The devaluation of any of these will help to alleviate global racially based economic disparities.

www.ingramcontent.com/pod-product-compliance
Lightning Source LLC
Chambersburg PA
CBHW060304290526
45789CB00001B/401